Walks in the Blue Mountains National Park

Sublime Point seen from the top of the Golden Stairs. The cliffs in the background are part of Kings Tableland

A HERITAGE FIELD GUIDE

Walks in the
BLUE MOUNTAINS
National Park

Neil Paton

Kangaroo Press

By the same author:

Treks in New South Wales
Sydney Bushwalks
Walks in the Sydney Harbour National Park

Reprinted 1989
First published in 1987 by Kangaroo Press Pty Ltd
3 Whitehall Road (P.O. Box 75) Kenthurst 2156
Typeset by T. & H. Bayfield
Printed by Australian Print Group, Maryborough 3465

ISBN 0-86417-129-3

Contents

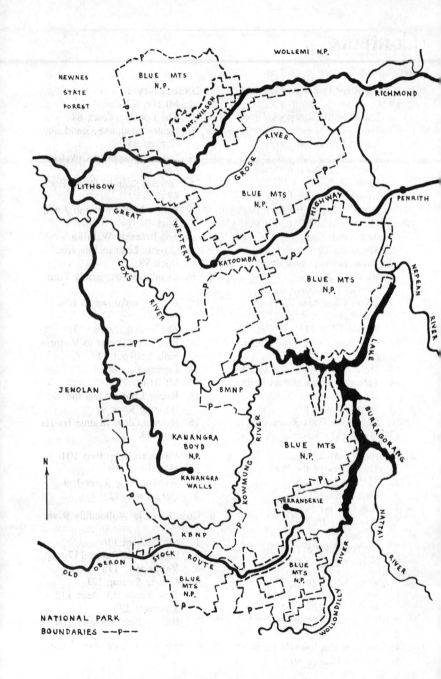

NATIONAL PARK
BOUNDARIES --P--

Introduction

The area now known as the Blue Mountains was created about a million years ago, when rocks were raised above the coastal plains to form a plateau of sandstone with layers of shale. Over the years, the plateau was dissected as rivers and creeks wore the sandstone layers away and exposed the shale below. The soft shale then collapsed, bringing layers of sandstone down with it and forming cliffs with slopes at the bottom where rubble piled up. The Hawkesbury sandstone, so characteristic of the whole Sydney region, created soil that was not especially fertile, so that the exposed ridges developed a rough covering of heath and dry schlerophyll forest. In the valleys and gullies, however, a moister and shadier world evolved, with waterfalls, cascades, ferns and pockets of magnificent rainforest.

This tangled maze of canyons and cliffs was home to Aboriginal tribes for many years, notably the Dharugs and Gundungaras. These people would have found the mountains a rich source of good, and have left their mark at numerous Aboriginal sites, including Red Hands Cave, Walls Cave and Du Faurs Rocks Lookout. To the early British settlers, however, the mountains presented a formidable barrier that was not quite the same as the hills and dales of Merry England. From the early days of the colony, the settlers probed and stabbed at the mountains but took twenty-five years to find a way across them. Captain Watkin Tench of the First Fleet travelled as far as the Nepean River, at the foot of the mountains, and was the first to realise that the Nepean and the Hawkesbury were one and the same. In 1791, Paterson followed up with an expedition that went from the Nepean and up the Grose River, getting perhaps as far as the junction with Wentworth Creek, but found the going too rough. If he had continued all the way up the river he would have come to the top of the Blue Mountains Range, near the present site of Bell, and would have been halfway across the mountains.

Bass, of Flinders fame, tried valiantly in 1796, penetrating the Burragorang Valley and making progress towards what is now known as Kanangra Range, but he was defeated by the rugged cliffs. An ex-convict, John Wilson, who had lived with the Aboriginals for some time, took a party of Irish convicts through the mountains in 1798, possibly getting as far as the vicinity of the Lachlan River. Unfortunately, his report and all records of his journey were lost for many years, but he may well have been the unrecognised conqueror of the mountains — no doubt because of his experience with the Aboriginals.

The Frenchman Barrallier took a similar path in 1802, starting from Nattai, which he had discovered, and penetrating the Burragorang Valley, Byrnes Gap and the Kowmung River. He went as far as Christys Creek, on the south side of Kanangra Tops, but, like Bass, he was defeated by the intimidating terrain. Anyone who goes to Kanangra today can imagine what it must have been like to tackle this kind of country without the benefit of maps and tracks.

Two years later, Caley led an expedition around the Grose River and up onto the Bell Range. He passed through tortuous country which he named the Devils Wilderness — a name still in use today — and finally managed to get as far as Mt Banks, but he made the same mistake others had made by going up and down gullies. If he had followed the crest of the Bell Range he would have got through, but from Mt Banks the way west appears to be straight across the insurmountable barrier of the Grose Valley.

After the experience of the early explorers, the consensus gradually formed that the only way through the mountains would be to stick to the ridges, and this was the strategy adopted in 1813 by Blaxland, Lawson and Wentworth. This trio, largely motivated by the desire to find grazing land for themselves, started from around the present site of Emu Plains and followed the Blue Mountains Range where the Great Western Highway is now found. They finally reached Mt York, just west of Mt Victoria, and knew they had found the way. Another man, Evans, was commissioned later in the same year to complete the journey begun by Blaxland, Lawson and Wentworth. Evans went further, eventually reaching Mt Pleasant near Bathurst, and the mountains were conquered — somewhat ironically, considering they had been home to the Aboriginals all along.

Cox began building the first road through the mountains only a year later, and completed it in 1815, but the steep slopes around Mt York were always something of a problem. This prompted Archibald Bell junior to make further explorations in 1823. Bell emulated Caley by reaching Mt Banks but improved on the effort by following the Bell Range further west until he came to Cox's road where it went through Hartley Vale. This provided an alternative route across the mountains, and Bell is commemorated today by Bells Line of Road, or the Bell Road as it is more popularly known.

In the 19th century, tracks were built to provide walking access to the main valleys on either side of the Blue Mountains Range. In some cases, men had to be lowered down the cliffs on ropes to look for ledges where tracks could be built. Thanks to their efforts, the Blue Mountains have largely been tamed and walkers can gain access to most parts of the area. A wonderland of mountains, canyons, gullies and rivers has been opened up to the general public, who need no more than sensible walking shoes and a reasonable degree of fitness in order to avail themselves of this world. The Blue Mountains National Park, dedicated in 1959 and covering over 200 000 hectares of land, provides protection for most of this country, making it possible for walkers to escape from the city and enjoy the mountain scenery for a few hours or several days if they wish. The greatest number of walking tracks is concentrated, not surprisingly, around the north and south flanks of the Blue Mountains Range, in places like the Jamison Valley, the Grose Valley and innumerable nooks and crannies like Mabel Falls Reserve, Terrace Falls and Henson Glen. Further afield, various tracks make it possible to penetrate for many miles to such places as Scotts Main Range, Kanangra, Yerranderie and the Wollondilly River, enabling fit walkers to do treks of a week or more. In the opposite direction, to the north, Mt Wilson exists as a little island of civilisation surrounded by the national park, but even within this island there are numerous tracks that open up some beautiful areas of rainforest, waterfalls and fern trees.

Beyond Mt Wilson, the rugged and largely untamed land of the Wallangambe Wilderness takes over, presenting experienced walkers with the opportunity to truly have this world to themselves if they are capable of finding their way through it. If they can go further, they can press beyond the boundary of the Blue Mountains National Park, at Railmotor Ridge, and into the forbidding territory of the Wollemi National Park, which will separate the bushwalking goats from the wandering sheep. From the ruggedness of the Wallangambe Wilderness to the tamer corners of the cliff tracks at the Jamison Valley, the Blue Mountains present a variety of scenery and walks that may be unequalled in this country; it is one of the greatest national parks of New South Wales and no doubt one of the great parks of Australia.

The following text — the first to cover the entire Blue Mountains National Park — is divided into six sections, allowing a detailed coverage of the park and its environs. Many of the areas described are suitable for beginners as well as more experienced walkers; where a particular area is only suited to experienced bushwalkers, appropriate warnings are given. For day-walks, the only equipment necessary is a sensible pair of walking shoes and some king of bag for carrying food. A topographic map and compass are also worth having, especially on longer walks. The maps required are mentioned in the text, and may be worth taking even on walks that appear to be quite straightforward.

1. Nepean River to Kings Tableland

To a certain extent this is the country of Blaxland, Lawson and Wentworth, who all owned land not far away on the east side of the Nepean, and who made their historic journey along the Blue Mountains Range which forms the northern edge of the area considered in this chapter. With the highway, railway line and built-up areas along the range, this section of the Blue Mountains has naturally been well developed with amenities and access roads, to the point where some consider it overdeveloped. A number of fire trails have been built along the ridges of this area, making for plenty of access but also for walks that are sometimes on the dull side. In spite of this, however, there are still many spots worth visiting. One of the most notable is the Portal Lookout, which provides superb views across the Nepean River, the Penrith Plains and all the way to Sydney. Further to the west, Glenbrook Creek provides scope for some worthwhile walks while Red Hands Cave is the site of a large number of Aboriginal hand stencils going back to the days of the Dharugs.

A number of picnic and camping areas have been developed at places like the Euroka Clearing, the Oaks, Tobys Glen and Murphys Glen, and provide some beautiful spots for family groups as well as bushwalkers. A range of fire trails and tracks links most of these places up with each other and also with Kings Tableland, at the bottom of which is McMahons Lookout. From this lookout there are spectacular views of Lake Burragorang, the Broken Rock Range and the southern part of the Jamison Valley, as well as an old service road that provides access to the lake and, for experienced bushwalkers, to the Jamison Valley via the prohibited zone around Lake Burragorang.

1. Lapstone to Glenbrook Creek

Opposite Lapstone Station, on the east side, is a fire trail that goes down the hill (turn south at the trail) and curves around to arrive at a cul-de-sac at the bottom (Lapstone Place). Just before reaching Lapstone Place, there is a foot-track on the east side of the trail. This leads along the banks of the Nepean River to emerge at the mouth of Glenbrook Creek — perhaps forty-five minutes' walk. This area, adjacent to the Nepean, is a pleasant place marred only by the noise of speed-boats and water skiers. This is a popular area on weekends and public holidays, so anyone wanting peace and quiet would be well advised to go there on weekdays. There is little by way of camping areas around here, although there are one or two

GLENBROOK, NEPEAN RIVER
FOOT-TRACK————
FIRE TRAIL ━━━━
C—CLEARING, CAMP SITE
P—PICNIC AREA
RHC—RED HANDS CAVE
GC—GLENBROOK CAUSEWAY
VC—VISITORS CENTRE
TVL—TUNNEL VIEW LOOKOUT
PL—PORTAL LOOKOUT
LP—LAPSTONE PLACE
EL—ERSKINE LOOKOUT
JE—JACK EVANS TRACK
NL—NEPEAN LOOKOUT

reasonable spots at the foot of Portal Mountain, where a track goes up to Portal Lookout, which will be discussed in Section 7.

2. Lower Glenbrook Creek

It is possible, of course, to follow Glenbrook Creek from the Nepean River up to Glenbrook Causeway, where the creek is crossed by the road from Glenbrook to the Oaks Fire Trail. There is no track and it is fairly slow going along the rocks. It took me about two and a half hours to go from the Causeway to the Nepean, carrying a backpack. About halfway along, there is a large rock shelter on the west side of the creek, and this could be used for camping. Unfortunately, it has already been defaced by the graffiti mob, who seem to be unable to control themselves when confronted by a blank expanse of sandstone. The water from the creek, of course, must be considered suspect, but can be drunk if boiled or chlorinated.

Just on the south side of the causeway is the Jelly Bean Pool, a popular swimming hole. A track leads down to the pool from the Glenbrook Road, near the Visitors Centre. Camping is prohibited at the Jelly Bean Pool.

It is possible to walk further upstream along Glenbrook Creek, but the old track, which is still shown on the Penrith Topographic map, is largely overgrown and the walking is fairly slow and rough. This is not a walk for anyone out for an easy Sunday stroll. Not far upstream of the Causeway, you come to the Blue Pool, another popular swimming hole which is also accessible via a track from the Glenbrook Road — shown on the Penrith topographic map. There is a beach where camping is possible if you do not mind camping on sand — the worst kind of surface for camping, in my experience.

Further on is the popular spot known as the Duckhole, and a couple of kilometres upstream of this is a track that goes to Blaxland. The track is found at a spot where the creek bends around in a westerly direction; on the east side there is a gully that comes down from the Blaxland area, and the track is to be found on the east side of this gully (not on the west side, as shown on the maps). The track follows the gully, criss-crossing it a bit, with one or two spots where you have to shimmy along a fallen log. It eventually emerges on the west side of the gully and joins a track that goes around the side of the hill. You will see a branch that goes straight up the hill, but this should be ignored, since it goes straight into the back of some houses. Turn east and follow the track around the hillside and after some fairly longwinded twists, through quite rich and pleasant bush, the track comes out near View Street, Blaxland. It splits into minor branches near the end, getting rather vague and taking you towards a few backyards if you are not careful. It is a pity that the council allowed residential development in places like this without taking the tracks into account. This whole stretch, from the Blue Pool to the Blaxland track, is quite slow and rough, as I said, and can be quite a solid day's walk with a backpack.

3. Upper Glenbrook Creek — Martins Lookout to Picnic Point

Martins Lookout is about four kilometres from Springwood Station, accessible via Farm Road. The road is unsealed for the last kilometre and a half, but is in good condition. At the end of the road there is a parking area, and a track that leads to the lookout. As you approach the lookout, you will find yourself facing a sign pointing left to the lookout, and the Long Track to Sassafras Gully. To the right, the sign points to the Short Track to Sassafras Gully. Proceed to the left and you will come to the rocky point that constitutes the lookout. The view from this point encompasses the gullies and hills around the upper part of Glenbrook Creek, but it is no big deal in my opinion, so I would not suggest that anyone should go there just for the sake of the view (although it might be better at sunset or sunrise). However, it is a good starting point for walks in the area.

To the east of the lookout, across the rocky ground, you will find the beginning of the Long Track to Glenbrook Creek. This track zig-zags very broadly down the slopes, making its way among numerous rock formations and overhangs. The track is in quite good condition and has plenty of steps where they are needed. Although it constitutes a slightly rocky and uneven surface in places, any average walker would have no trouble. At the bottom of the slope, the track comes close to the creek and smooths out and widens considerably. The forest, naturally, is much greener and richer than it is up the top; before long, the track, continuing upstream, reaches a long clearing that would make a good place to camp. You will see the remains of people's camp-fires, and nearby there are some decent pools that make a nice spot for a lunch-break or a dip at the right time of year.

The track continues upstream, climbing the slopes slightly and undulating somewhat. It is in generally good condition although getting slightly overgrown here and there; whether it will be as good in ten years is open to debate, unless some upgrading is done.

About a third of a kilometre along, you come to the bottom of the Short Track, which similarly is in reasonable condition and has numerous steps where needed. There are some sign-posts on a tree at the bottom of the

Short Track; from this point, you continue upstream along the undulating track, sometimes close to the edge of the creek, sometimes further up the slope, until you cross the rocky mouth of Magdala Creek, which comes in roughly from the north. On the west side, there is another clearing that could be used for camping, and a track going to the north as well as the continuation of the main track along Glenbrook Creek. This spot is known as Perch Ponds, the Ponds in question being a few little pools along Glenbrook Creek.

From Perch Ponds, the main track continues to Faulconbridge, but for the moment we shall consider the track to the north, since this makes a good afternoon's walk in its own right. There are sign-posts around here which indicate that the track to the north goes to Homedale Street, which is in Springwood, although it would have been more pertinent to say 'Picnic Point' or 'Valley Road'. Carping aside, however, the track proceeds immediately up the slope and follows the gully of Magdala Creek, several metres above the creek itself. It continues along the foot of some attractive cliffs, decorated with ferns, and before long brings you to a large pool where you will see Martin Falls (although I hope you find more water in them than I did).

A few minutes' walk upstream of Martins Falls, the track passes the Blue Pool. A minor turn-off leaves the track to go to a spot where you have a good view of the pool, although I did not see any easy way to get down to it. The walls around the pool are quite steep, and the pool itself has more than its share of semi-submerged logs, making it risky to dive in. Even

The Blue Pool, Glenbrook Creek, after heavy rain

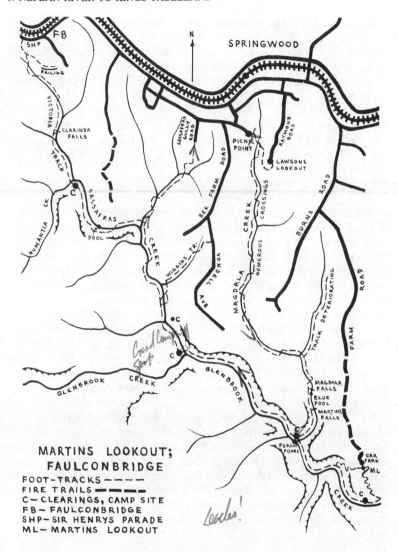

MARTINS LOOKOUT;
FAULCONBRIDGE
FOOT-TRACKS - - - -
FIRE TRAILS ▬ ▬ ▬ ▬
C - CLEARINGS, CAMP SITE
FB - FAULCONBRIDGE
SHP - SIR HENRYS PARADE
ML - MARTINS LOOKOUT

A bit further upstream of the Blue Pool, the track passes another pool and then crosses the creek at a wide, rocky stretch. After a few minutes' if you dived in and survived, you might have trouble getting back up to the track. The pool lives up to its name and is very blue, as well as being graced with its own waterfall — Magdala Falls; it is worth taking in.

walk on the other side — the east side — you come to a turn-off to the left, where there is a metal arrow attached to a tree. The arrow has the letters RYLA written on it, but I am not sure what they mean. The track on the east side continues upstream for a while but eventually comes to a dead-end, as shown on the Springwood topographic map, and is getting overgrown.

From the metal sign, you cross to the west to continue up the gully of Magdala Creek, then cross again and pass some attractive rock shelters. The track is very clear along this stretch, while the bush has changed to more of a dry eucalypt scrub, in contrast to the more lush undergrowth along some parts of the creek.

From here on, there are numerous creek crossings that are not worth describing in detail. By and large, they are quite clear and straightforward, so that no-one need have any trouble. Eventually you pass under the first of a few sets of power-lines that cross the gully, and on the east side the track takes you back into more lush, rainforesty nooks and crannies, with moss-covered rock shelters that create very attractive, cloistered surroundings. After crossing a wooden footbridge you go uphill slightly and come to the turn-off for Lawsons Lookout. This track is sign-posted and zig zags up the slope to the east to arrive at the lookout, which is, in my humble opinion, even more of a non-event than Martins Lookout. From the lookout, a track leads to the bottom of Raymond Road, Springwood. It is only about ten minutes' walk from the main track up to the lookout.

From the turn-off for Lawsons Lookout, you cross another wooden footbridge and gradually proceed uphill, via stone steps, to arrive at Picnic Point. This is a small picnic area with shelter, water-tank and fire-place, set in a small park. The track comes out on the east side of the park, and is not sign-posted. From the park, an unsealed road leads up to the east end of Valley Road, and from there it is only about ten minutes' walk to Springwood Station. The walk from Martins Lookout to Picnic Point is quite an enjoyable afternoon's walk which any average walker could do in four hours without trouble. I have found that it can take twice as long to cover ground on these tracks as it might on a road, so it is as well to use this as a yardstick when planning the walk, although four hours is a likely time, in this case, for any reasonably fit walker.

4. Upper Glenbrook Creek — Perch Ponds to Faulconbridge

This is quite possibly the most pleasant walk around Glenbrook Creek. The track passes through a considerable variety of scenery, with some beautiful spots to be enjoyed. From Perch Ponds, the track continues much as before, undulating a fair bit, going uphill for a while and eventually working its way back down to the edge of the creek. After about five minutes' walk, you pass a good, wide pool that would be a welcome sight in summer; the pool has a strong, blue-green colour that is characteristic of the pools in this area. Further along, the track, which is in quite good condition, passes by the foot of a beautiful cliff, which is shown on the Springwood topographic map, and through some pleasant ferny areas before going back down to the creek.

After walking for twenty minutes or so you come to the junction of Glenbrook and Sassafras Creeks, where there is another large pool, although a fairly shallow one. On the west side of the junction there is a large clearing that would make a good camp-site, although there is no excess of firewood. A tree in the clearing is endowed with some signs — an old one and a new one — pointing the way to Springwood, Faulconbridge and Sassafras Gully Road.

The track now continues upstream along Sassafras Creek, and has been given the name Victoria Track. From this point, it gets a bit patchier and there are some spots where it is beginning to get mildly overgrown. At the time of writing there were no difficulties, but within ten years I think this track could be quite messy in places if no work is done on it.

A few minutes' walk upstream from the junction of the creeks, you pass a small clearing that can be seen on the east side of Sassafras Creek; this could naturally be used for camping, although the one at the junction is far superior. After another five or ten minutes you come to a fork in the track; the branch to the east goes down and crosses the creek to join the Wiggins Track to Yondell Avenue, Springwood. The turn-off from the Victoria Track is not sign-posted; if heading for the Wiggins Track, cross the creek and turn upstream, since in the downstream direction there is another branch that simply goes back to the creek at a spot where there is a wooden footbridge, and then rejoins the Victoria Track. It is all rather intriguing, and no doubt helped to create jobs for someone.

The Victoria Track gets fairly narrow and mildly overgrown in places along this stretch, but also extremely pleasant, with trees and bushes sheltering the track to create a cool, cloistered atmosphere. A little upstream of the Wiggins Track turn-off, the track crosses to the east side of the creek and before long you will notice the first set of power-lines that go overhead on their way to Faulconbridge and beyond. Another five minutes' walk brings you to the track to Sasafras Gully Road, where there is another sign-post. Turning directly west, you continue along the main track and come to another creek crossing. About five minutes' walk further upstream, there is a minor branch that leads down to a good pool on Sassafras Creek. This pool, too, has the strong blue-green colouring seen before. After this it is only ten minutes' walk or so to the junction of Sassafras and Numantia Creeks, on the south side of which you will find another large clearing that would make an excellent camp ground. All the watercourses in this area seem to come from built-up areas and could be polluted to some degree, so if you camp around here you should be prepared to boil or chlorinate your drinking water.

From the above junction, the track goes uphill for a while before going back down to cross a gully, in a pattern that is characteristic of this track — up the slope, along for a while and then down again at the next gully. Going up again after crossing a small stream, the track comes to the vicinity of Clarinda Falls, one of the most beautiful spots along Sassafras Creek. You will see where a minor branch turns off to the east side of the main track, with a log blocking the turn-off. This turn-off leads to Clarinda Falls, which flow down into a small, semi-circular amphitheatre. The walls of the amphitheatre are bedecked with layer upon layer of ferns and thick moss, combining with the innumerable trickles of water to create a beautiful display that is one of the highlights of the walk. The creek immediately downstream of the falls is also a pleasant sight, richly decorated with ferns. When I was there the place was free of litter and in pretty pristine condition; one can only beg people to keep it that way.

From the turn-off to the falls, the main track climbs up the slopes above the falls and goes through some dry eucalypt forest that is quite a contrast to other parts of the gully; after this, the track goes downhill again and crosses the creek at a shady little nook that heralds the return to the rainforest environment found in places along the bottom of the gully. This kind of variety and contrast make the walk an interesting one.

After crossing to the east side of the creek, you find yourself in a beautiful rainforest pocket, and a little further along there is a particularly atmospheric section where the track passes some good rock shelters. Rock formations loom over the track and a fallen tree creates a natural arch, leading into a little world that may be shortlived, but which I personally found beautiful and fascinating.

From this rainforest pocket, the track gradually begins to wind its way uphill, meandering among the rocks until it eventually comes to another set of rock shelters further up the slope. Two rock shelters are found side by side, serviced by a minor track and obviously popular with the local kids, to judge by the graffiti. The main track then goes above these rock shelters and comes to a dead-end branch that is shown on the Springwood map and which goes for about a hundred metres to the south-east before fizzling out. It is adorned, further along, by some rusty iron railings that were obviously put there to stop people from dropping off the edge. The railings are in a state of collapse and should not be leaned on for safety reasons.

From this branch, the main track continues gradually up the slopes, passing through the usual dry eucalypt scrub before arriving at Sir Henry Parade, Faulconbridge, opposite no. 32. There is a red sign saying 'Springwood' at the beginning of the track, and from there it is only five minutes' walk to Faulconbridge Station, concluding a superb walk that must be one of the best that can be done in this part of the Blue Mountains. It took me about three hours to walk from Perth Ponds to Faulconbridge, going fairly briskly; it would be best to allow more time to do it at a leisurely pace.

5. Red Hands Cave

On the north side of Glenbrook Causeway there is a sign-posted track to the Red Hands Cave, a rock shelter with Aboriginal hand stencils. A wire fence has been put across the mouth of the shelter to give the stencils some protection from vandalism. There is quite a large number of stencils, mostly in red or brownish colouring, and including the hands of children as well as adults.

Above the cave, the track goes to a basic picnic area with water-tank, although the tank was empty when I was there, and from the picnic area continues on to the Red Hands Fire Trail. The track is in good condition all the way from Glenbrook Creek. On the other hand, to follow the track up Camp Fire Creek instead of turning off for Red Hands Cave is quite a different matter. This track is overgrown and presents quite a rough walk. Up at the picnic area near Red Hands Cave, there is a sign pointing the way to Glenbrook via the track along Camp Fire Creek, but unfortunately it does not say how badly the track has deteriorated (unless it has been upgraded recently, which I doubt).

6. The Oaks

The Red Hands Fire Trail leads down to the Oaks Camp Ground, which of course can also be reached via the Oaks Fire Trail, starting either at Woodford or Glenbrook. This camp ground had been closed for an unconscionably long time to allow for regeneration and restoration after the drought of the early eighties. Anyone thinking of camping there should phone the Visitors Centre at Glenbrook for the latest information. A ranger told me they were considering closing the camp ground to vehicles and restricting it entirely to backpackers. Personally, I think it would be a good idea if they closed the whole area to vehicles. The camp ground, in any case, is quite spacious, and there is a watertank across the road.

7. Portal Lookout and Euroka Clearing

Two major points of interest in the eastern section are the Euroka Clearing and the Portal Lookout. The latter is on top of Portal Mountain and can be reached by car via a turn-off from the Oaks Fire Trail, or on foot from the mouth of Glenbrook Creek. If you drive from the Oaks Fire Trail, the last stretch of the road is a little rough and there is a sign suggesting that cars should be left at that point. Most people do this, although it looked to me that a normal car could probably handle the road if taken carefully; it is possible, of course, that the road could have deteriorated more recently. If you leave the car behind, a walk of about one kilometre is necessary to reach the lookout. It is, of course, well worth it, for the Portal offers one of the best views you are likely to see for a while. The view takes in the Nepean River, Glenbrook Gorge, Penrith, the Penrith Plains and even the City of Sydney on the horizon. It is even possible to make out the Centrepoint Tower if you look carefully. This is a great place to watch the sun come up, although I do not know how the National Parks and Wildlife Service feels about people camping at the lookout. There are certainly no facilities there, and the nearest water is at the Portal Waterhole, about two kilometres back down the road, on a minor turn-off.

For those who do not mind a steep walk, the lookout can also be reached via a foot-track from Glenbrook Creek. The track can be found a hundred metres or so upstream from the mouth of Glenbrook Creek, at the foot of Portal Mountain, near a clearing that would suffice for camping. At the top of the track you are faced with a bit of a rock-climb which is not as daunting as it first looks, since there are several excellent foot-holds and hand-holds. If you are carrying a backpack, however, it would be advisable to take a rope for hauling the pack. This would be a good place for a steel ladder, if anyone would like to install one.

The Euroka Clearing is south-east of the Portal Lookout and can be reached via a turn-off from the Oaks Fire Trail. It has all the look of a private farm that has reverted to public use; it is a popular spot for family camping, with plenty of open, grassy space, water-tanks and so forth. However, it is necessary to book in advance at the Glenbrook Visitors Centre. This is the kind of place that appeals to family groups who like to almost set up house in the bush, but it gets crowded on weekends and public holidays and would probably not appeal as much to the hardy bushwalker species.

8. Nepean Lookout Area

On the south side of the Oaks Camp Ground is the road to the Nepean Lookout, which is about five kilometres to the south-east. This lookout offers views of the Nepean Gorge but is not a patch on the Portal Lookout in my humble opinion. Some points along the way are the Attic Cave and Machins

The view of the Nepean River from Nepean Lookout

Crater; there is also, just before the lookout, the Erskine Creek Camp Ground. I have found this a pleasant place to camp, since you have a fairly open western aspect and can get the benefit of the sunset. From the camp ground, a track leads to Erskine Creek Lookout, which is nothing to write home about, and then down to Erskine Creek, which is a much more interesting place, especially if you want to cool off in summer. On the other side of the creek, near the junction with Big Crater Creek, the Jack Evans Track leads up to the Warragamba Watershed Fire Trail, which in turn goes all the way to the Kings Tableland Road. This opens up the possibility of some quite long walks; I confess I have not gone along this trail, but from my experience of fire trails in this area there is a chance it could be a bit monotonous in parts.

9. Tobys Glen Area

From the Oaks Camp Ground, the Oaks Fire Trail continues for about six kilometres before reaching Tobys Glen, one of the more pleasant spots in the area. A turn-off with a locked gate goes downhill and does a loop through the glen, providing a little tour of a very secluded, green and pleasant sanctuary that would be a good place to spend a night. There are fire-places provided, plus a water-hole.

A little further north of Tobys Glen, the road takes a sharp turn to the east and there is a spot where you can get good views across the Penrith Plains. A rough fire-place can be seen at the spot; after this, it is an uneventful seven kilometres into Woodford.

10. Murphys Glen Area

Unfortunately, there is no foot-track connecting the Oaks Fire Trail with Murphys Glen, but experienced walkers could consider a scrub-bash from the road, starting around the abovementioned sharp turn to the east and going down the slope to Bedford Creek. The slope has some steep, rocky sections that have to be negotiated carefully; once down at the creek, you can walk upstream for about a kilometre and pick up a track that goes up to Murphys Glen. The track is marked on the Jamison topographic map, but goes a little further east than is shown; it can be found on the edge of Coolana Brook, which joins Bedford Creek at a decent-sized pool. This walk from the Oaks Fire Trail to Coolana Brook is quite rough and is strictly for experienced walkers. The track, once found, goes through some pleasant

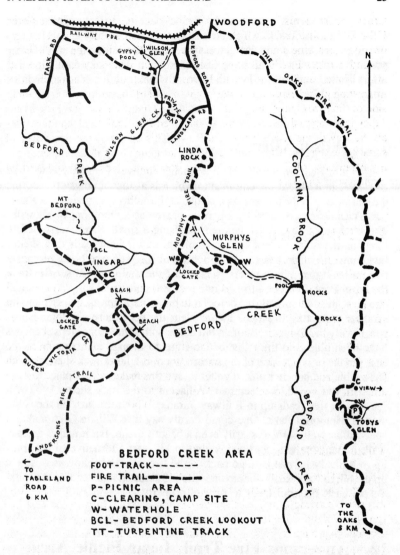

BEDFORD CREEK AREA
FOOT-TRACK - - - - - -
FIRE TRAIL ━━━━━━━
P-PICNIC AREA
C-CLEARING, CAMP SITE
W-WATERHOLE
BCL-BEDFORD CREEK LOOKOUT
TT-TURPENTINE TRACK

nooks and crannies as it goes up the gully to Murphys Glen where it goes past a pool and into the main camping area.

Murphys Glen is a pleasant enough area, but unfortunately it has been flogged to death. There is very little firewood, and you may have the misfortune of being entertained by local juveniles on trail bikes. On weekdays, however, it can still be a nice place. One feature of the area is the Turpentine Track, which goes from the camp ground up to Murphys Fire Trail, passing some distinctive turpentine trees along the way. Going north, Murphys Fire Trail passes Linda Rock, a flat rocky formation that offers limited views of the Penrith Plains; the fire trail then leads to Bedford Road, Woodford.

11. Wilson Glen

Just west of Bedford Road, where it reaches Railway Parade, you will see Buena Vista Road, at the entrance to which is a stone archway that forms the entrance to Wilson Glen. As a plaque at the archway explains, a walking track was developed here by a private citizen as a memorial to his wife. The track goes down into the glen, crossing a small watercourse before long; on the other side of the watercourse, an offshoot leads to a shelter just above the main track. At the bottom of the glen, the track reaches a fire trail and just a little further west along the trail you will see the track to Gypsy Pool. The pool itself is rather slight, consisting simply of a small stream with some logs placed across it to build the water up. No-one should go there expecting to have a swim. Near the pool there are some ruins, specifically the foundations of an old home with some stone steps; benches have been placed in the midst of the ruins to form a rudimentary picnic site. On the opposite side of the stream, there is a large rock shelter which has a table and benches placed under it, and this makes a cool place to have a rest if you go there in summer. Adjacent to the rock shelter, you will see a track that leads up to Railway Parade, Woodford, just on the south side of Memorial Park. One could hardly say that Wilson Glen makes a spectacular walk, or necessarily even a beautiful one, but it makes an easy walk for anyone with an hour or two to kill. An alternative to the track up to Railway Parade is to go back to the fire trail and follow it west and up the hill to Park Road, for anyone who is interested in extending the walk. To the east, the trail leads to private property.

12. Andersons Fire Trail, Ingar Picnic Area

From near Murphys Glen, a fire trail leads down to Bedford Creek and continues roughly south-east to Kings Tableland Road. This is quite a reasonable walk, with more interest and variety than is often the case on such fire trails. After fording Bedford Creek, the trail goes downstream

a little and fords Queen Victoria Creek before going uphill onto Notts Ridge.
This ford is described on the Jamison topographic map as a 'washout' for
some reason, but is actually just another ford. After going up the slopes
and onto the ridge, it is a very meandering walk of about eight kilometres
to get to the Tableland Road, arriving about a kilometre north of the High
Valley property — not a bad walk for anyone who wants an easy walk of
a few days or so, from Woodford to, say, Wentworth Falls, via Murphys
Glen, Bedford Creek and the Tablelands Road. There is a small beach at
the junction of Queen Victoria Creek and Bedford Creek, and this makes
a nice spot to camp, although firewood is a little scarce. Once again, this
area is to be preferred on weekdays.

On the west side of the ford at Bedford Creek, there is a fire trail that
goes up to Ingar Picnic Area, which also has a camping area. On the north
side of Ingar, there is a walking track that goes to Bedford Creek Lookout
— again, nothing to write home about — and Mt Bedford, doing a loop
back to the picnic area, making an easy afternoon's stroll. To be blunt about
it, I found Ingar a rather dry and uninteresting place. As one of the locals
said to me, 'This place is like a river that's been fished out'. The place
nevertheless makes a reasonable day-walk for anyone spending a couple
of nights at Murphys Glen.

13. McMahons Lookout Area

This lookout is found at the bottom of Kings Tableland Road, about twenty-
nine kilometres from Wentworth Falls Station. It provides spectacular views
of Lake Burragorang and the ranges in the southern part of the Blue
Mountains National Park, particularly the Broken Rock Range; plus views
to the west, featuring Narrow Neck Plateau and the Wild Dog Mountains.
There are a couple of picnic spots near the end of the road, the first of
them right beside the road and the second a bit further west, on the way
to the 'alternative lookout', which is sign-posted. The rangers do not seem
to mind people camping at these spots.

The lookout itself is about ten minutes' walk from the end of the road
(the sign rather cautiously says 'one hour'). Just before reaching the lookout,
you will see where the main track bears left, ie east; this is the old road
that went through the Burragorang Valley before Warragamba Dam was
built. It is possible to follow the road down to the lake, although doing so
involves going into the prohibited zone that extends for about three
kilometres around Lake Burragorang (all in the interest of protecting
Sydney's water supply, although at the time of writing the Water Board

is debating whether to open the area up to the public). The road has deteriorated badly and a bit of clambering is necessary in some places; it is also necessary to crawl on hands and knees in one or two spots because the road is getting so overgrown in places, and at times it is no more than a rough foot-track.

I suggest you give yourself a full day for the walk down to the lake, since it can be more time-consuming than expected. Take note of how long it takes you to reach the lake and allow yourself plenty of time to get back before dark, taking into account the fact that the return trip will be longer because it is uphill and you may be tired. Do not get stuck on this track at the end of the day, because it is a little vague in places and you would have no hope of following it in the dark, even with a strong torch.

Experienced walkers could consider going down to the lake and following it west a few kilometres to pick up a service trail that goes up to Kedumba Farm, in the Jamison Valley, and then to Wentworth Falls. The Water Board should be consulted about the latest conditions for permits for walking through the prohibited area.

The Kings Tableland Road can be a little monotonous from the point of view of a bushwalker, so that McMahons Lookout is best approached by car from around Wentworth Falls. There are a few points of interest along the way. About one and a half kilometres south of the 'High Valley' property, it is possible to leave the road and scrub-bash west to the edge of the tableland, where there are excellent views of the Jamison Valley. The scrub-bash is not difficult, as long as you stay out of the gully nearby, although only experienced walkers would want to bother. This would be a good place for a foot-track, if anyone feels like building one.

Further south is Harris Hill, which I personally have never got around to climbing, but which is clear on top and would probably provide some good views towards the Jamison. It is not steep and should be no trouble to climb, although I know of no track.

The next stop, a bit further south, is the Blue Drum Waterhole, which is the only reliable supply of water that I know of in the area. If you follow the service trail to the edge of the cliff there are some views of the Jamison, but it is hardly worth the walk because there are power-lines cluttering up the view. It would be possible to camp near the waterhole and, for that matter, in the clear spaces around some of the power-line towers. About a kilometre further south of the Blue Drum turn-off, there is a good camp-site on the west side of the main road, where a short turn-off leads to a large rock formation where there is a clearing and plenty of firewood.

14. Terrace Falls, Cataract Falls

Some of the most beautiful nooks and crannies in the Blue Mountains can be found near Hazelbrook and Lawson. Since many of these places are as little known as they are beautiful, it is tempting to keep them a secret and protect them from marauding litterbugs and vandals. However, as usual I have opted to inform people rather than give them the mushroom treatment, partly because the more people there are who know about them, the more potential pressure there is to preserve these places. Most of the places described in this section are not inside the Blue Mountains National Park, for some strange reason, and one can only hope they will, in the long run, receive the protection they deserve.

A good place to start exploring this area is Hazelbrook Station, from where you should walk west along Railway Parade until you come to Terrace Falls Road, the second street on your left (the Katoomba topographic map is handy for these walks). Follow Terrace Falls Road straight down and you will soon be in the bush. About a kilometre down, on the west side, you will see some ruins (no more than foundations) surrounded nicely by pine trees. Further along, there are some sharp bends in the road and a rough camp-site will be seen near some minor watercourses, before you arrive at a turn-off on the east side. This is Lake Road, which goes up to Valley Road. At the junction of Lake Road and Terrace Falls Road, there are some picnic facilities in the form of sheltered tables and chairs plus, on the west side of the road, some open space that could be used for camping.

Not much further south, a fire trail branches off on the west side of Terrace Falls Road. This leads up to Cataract Falls, but for the moment you should look for a foot-track that branches off the fire trail immediately before it fords the creek that lies ahead. This creek has no name to my knowledge, but for convenience I will call it Terrace Falls Creek. Follow this track downstream and look for a spot where the track crosses the creek just before Victor Falls (you will see all this on the Katoomba map). The crossing is not particularly conspicuous; there is an old, faded sign on a tree, but the sign is just as inconspicuous as the crossing itself.

Nevertheless, having crossed the creek, follow the track as it goes slightly uphill and south, until it bends around and begins the descent to the gully of Terrace Falls Creek. Part of the way down, there is a branch on your left which leads to Victor Falls. This is worth having a look at, even if the spot has been slightly marred by the presence of an old water-tank. It is a dead-end track, so you will have to retrace your steps to the main track after you have seen Victor Falls. Up until reaching this branch, the track is quite reasonable, but from here on it gets a little overgrown and cluttered in places, without presenting any serious difficulties.

The beautiful Terrace Falls, outside Hazelbrook

Back on the main track, continue south, cross the creek a bit further along and you soon come to Terrace Falls. A minor turn-off goes down to the falls, which are worth a good, long look. These falls descend in several stages — or terraces — and are quite beautiful, as is the whole area. Near the turn-off to the falls you will see a track that goes uphill and back to Terrace Falls Road, where it is clear enough but not sign-posted. Ignore this track and continue downstream along the main track. The gully by this time is full of fern and is quite a beautiful, atmospheric place. A little further along, the track crosses back to the west side of the creek, and at this point

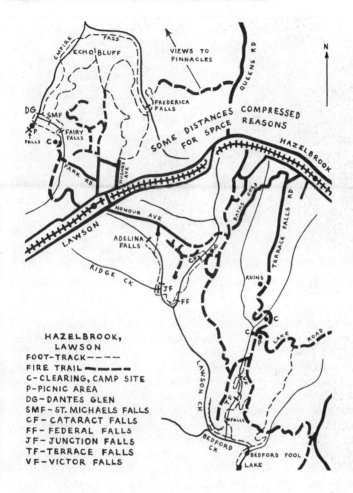

HAZELBROOK,
LAWSON
FOOT-TRACK----
FIRE TRAIL ▬ ▬ ▬ ▬
C - CLEARING, CAMP SITE
P - PICNIC AREA
DG - DANTES GLEN
SMF - ST. MICHAELS FALLS
CF - CATARACT FALLS
FF - FEDERAL FALLS
JF - JUNCTION FALLS
TF - TERRACE FALLS
VF - VICTOR FALLS

you have a particularly peaceful, beautiful spot. An old, moss-covered log leans against the rocks while the creek falls softly behind it — a spot I always found particularly magical. Before long, the track crosses again to the east side of the creek at a spot where there is an unnamed waterfall. After this, it continues through rich forest until it begins to bear east as the gully widens and Terrace Falls Creek merges with Bedford Creek. Here the area becomes more open and you come to a sign-posted turn-off that leads back up to Terrace Falls Road.

Immediately downstream of this turn-off is a bit of a pool, described as

A scene along Bedford Creek

Cliff formations in the vicinity of Bedford Creek

Bedford Pool on the map. Crossing Bedford Creek to the west side, you will see some stone steps that lead to a track that goes further downstream to a long pool described on the abovementioned sign-post as a lake. The track fizzles out on a rocky stretch alongside the lake. This track was shown on the old Katoomba map but was unfortunately left off the new one. The more adventurous could do a scrub-bash up the slopes from the abovementioned stone steps, and join the fire trails that link up with Murphys Fire Trail. From there it is possible to go west to the Kings Tableland Road or east to Ingar Picnic ground and even Murphys Glen, thus opening up the possibility of several extended walks beginning in Hazelbrook and going as far as you wish to go.

For our present purposes, however, let us return to the fire trail that fords Terrace Falls Creek and continues to Cataract Falls. Follow this fire trail uphill and north, take the first turn-off to your left and you are soon at the picnic ground adjacent to Cataract Falls. On the west side of the picnic ground, a track fords Cataract Creek and takes you to a lookout from which you can look down at the falls; the track then continues west to Broad Street, Lawson. However, the better idea is to take the track that you will find on the south side of the picnic ground and follow it downstream. A minor turn-off a little further down gives you a worm's-eye view of Cataract Falls. You pass some more basic picnic facilities, of which there is a plentiful supply in the area. After crossing the creek further downstream, you will see the turn-off for Federal Falls, another spot worth looking at before carrying on. There are so many waterfalls in this area that the whole walk could be called the Waterfall Walk. Anyone who likes viewing, or photographing, waterfalls will have their fill on this walk, although so much depends, of course, on rainfall.

Bending around north-west, the track goes upstream along Lawson Creek and arrives at Junction Falls, so-called because of the waterfalls at the junction of Ridge Creek and Lawson Creek. The whole spot is worth taking in, but the falls on Ridge Creek are the more spectacular of the two.

From this point the track starts to go uphill and the scrub becomes drier as you go towards Lawson. Further north, you find a minor turn-off on your left and this leads to Adelina Falls — the smallest waterfall on the walk. A run-down bench provides the inevitable picnic facilities for those who want them, although it is hardly a beautiful picnic spot. After this, it is simply a matter of continuing to the east side of Lawson Creek and following the track uphill to a cul-de-sac that leads to Broad Street, on the outskirts of Lawson. Turning left, or north, along Broad Street, you soon find yourself at Honour Avenue, which leads to Honour Gardens. These gardens feature trees planted to commemorate individual soldiers who died in the First World War. Honour Gardens lead to the Great Western Highway, more or less opposite Lawson Station. A fit walker could do the entire circuit, from Hazelbrook to Bedford Creek and up to Lawson, in four hours or so without straining.

15. Empire Pass

Further exploration of the Lawson area continues by crossing to the north side of the tracks and going down San Jose Avenue. Turn left at Park Avenue, and at the bottom of the hill you will find a large and spacious camp ground that makes an excellent place to spend the night for anyone who wants to do an overnight walk in the area. Water is available from the small stream on the east side of the camp ground, although it is probably best to boil or chlorinate it. Following the dirt road that goes along the east side of the camp ground, you will pick up the sign-posted track that goes down into Dantes Glen and continues as the beautiful Empire Pass. Before going down into the glen, you will see a waterfall called Fairy Falls, and will also see where the track — or a branch of it — crosses the creek just below the falls. This branch leads to a lookout from which you have a good view of the waterfall, although you have a perfectly good view of it in the first place. This turn-off can be followed around to Echo Bluff, Frederica Falls and back to Lawson, but for the moment let us descend to Dantes

Glen. This involves going down some stone steps that might make for a steep walk if you were going the other way, but in the walk as suggested there are no terribly steep slopes.

Dantes Glen is a beautiful place with its own waterfall, ferns and the usual tables and benches. From Dantes Glen the walk continues along a ferny, shady creek that appears to have no name. Before long you come to the sign-posted turn-off for St Michael's Falls, which are worth having a look at. You must cross the creek at this point to stay with the main track. It appears to keep going on the original side for a while, but eventually fizzles out and it is then necessary to do a scrub-bash up the slope to find the main track again. I should add that the Katoomba map is wrong at this point in showing the track entirely on the east side of the creek; you cross to the west side at Dantes Glen and re-cross to the east for St Michaels Falls as well as to follow the main track.

From here the track climbs slightly uphill for a while before eventually going back down and crossing the creek to continue once more on the west. The scenery around the creek is very lush and beautiful, and it is a pity the track was not built alongside the creek all the way. A little further along, there is a junction with a creek that flows down from Frederica Falls. Just before this junction, the track again crosses to the east side and makes its way gradually uphill. You start to get into more of a eucalypt scrub as you get up the slopes, although still with some decent fern trees, until eventually you come to Frederica Falls, a pleasant spot with its own set of picnic facilities. On the opposite side of the creek you will see another track, which leads to Queens Road, Hazelbrook. Along this track it is possible to make out the shapes of Flat Top and the Pinnacles up on the Mt Hay Road. From Frederica Falls you therefore have a choice of following the main track south to Hughes Avenue and back to Lawson; crossing the creek and going through to Queens Road; or taking the turn-off that leads to Echo Bluff. The main track to Hughes Avenue was closed at the Hughes Avenue end when I last saw it — due, apparently, to erosion — but could still be used from Frederica Falls.

16. Horseshoe Falls Reserve

Unfortunately, there is no connecting track from the Empire Pass to the next area of interest, Horseshoe Falls Reserve, which is accessible from Oaklands Road, Hazelbrook, on the north side of the Great Western Highway. To start at Oaklands Road, you will find a park on the south side of a stream just before the road bends west and becomes Hall Parade. The park is on the east side of Oaklands Road and there is an old, dilapidated

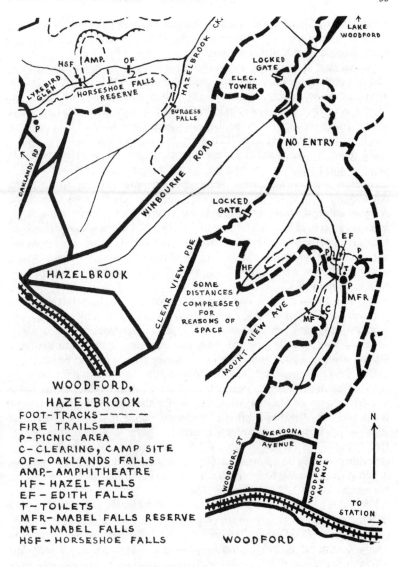

WOODFORD,
HAZELBROOK
FOOT-TRACKS ———
FIRE TRAILS ■■■■
P — PICNIC AREA
C — CLEARING, CAMP SITE
OF — OAKLANDS FALLS
AMP. — AMPHITHEATRE
HF — HAZEL FALLS
EF — EDITH FALLS
T — TOILETS
MFR — MABEL FALLS RESERVE
MF — MABEL FALLS
HSF — HORSESHOE FALLS

sign saying Horseshoe Falls Reserve. In the park there is an equally
dilapidated shelter with table and chairs, in case you feel like having lunch.
It is a shame to see how run-down and neglected the walks are in this area.
There are some beautiful places to be seen, and with characteristic Australian

reticence we have neglected them and kept them a secret. Perhaps the local council is dominated by conservationists who want to protect the beauty spots from us larrikin members of the public.

Be that as it may, on the north side of the reserve, alongside the stream, you will pick up the track that goes along the stream and into Lyrebird Glen. There are a few falls and cascades along the way before you come to the most spectacular spot, Horseshoe Falls. At this spot there is a large rock shelter that curves around in the shape of a horseshoe, from which I presume the falls derived their name. This spot is worth a close look.

On the east side of the falls, and the north side of the creek, you can pick up the track that goes to the Amphitheatre. This is a curved cliff formation which is a pleasant, ferny spot, but whether it is worth going out of your way to see is, I suppose, debatable. On the east side of the Amphitheatre, the track curves back down south but then becomes scrappy and overgrown, at least at the time of writing. Whether any restoration will have taken place by the time you read this is anybody's guess, but I would not count on it. In any case, I was unable to follow this track down to where it rejoins the main track through Lyrebird Glen, and had to double back to Horseshoe Falls.

From Horseshoe Falls, continue downstream and a little further along you will find Oaklands Falls, another pleasant spot worth a bit of your time. After that, the track continues along the slopes and approaches Burgess Falls. A minor track branches off the main one and goes upstream to the falls. On the way, you pass under a rock shelter bearing a plaque dedicated to L/Cpl E. A. Burgess, who died in World War One and after whom the falls are named. This is a beautiful spot well worth looking at, as much for the scenery of Hazelbrook Creek as for the waterfall. From around Burgess Falls, the track climbs gradually uphill to finally emerge at Winbourne Road. At Hazelbrook Station there is a sign saying that Horseshoe Falls Reserve can be reached via Winbourne Road, but unfortunately they do not mention the fact that the track is virtually invisible if you do not know where to look. It can be found beside a large tree on the north side of 122 Winbourne Road.

From this point you can go south to return to Hazelbrook, but the more intrepid might like to turn north and look for a fire trail on the east side of Winbourne Road, about ten minutes' walk further up. This trail was shown on the old Katoomba topographic map, but was unfortunately left off the new version. It goes east through the scrub and terminates at a steel tower where some power-lines go down the hill and through to Linden. The power-lines are shown on the map even if the trail is not. From where the trail terminates, it is a simple scrub-bash directly east and down the slope to join a service road that goes through to Lake Woodford. This is

Oaklands Falls, one of the features of
Horseshoe Falls Reserve

Burgess Falls, perhaps the most beautiful spot in Horseshoe Falls Reserve

prohibited area, due to the dam at the lake, so turn south and up the slope; about three-quarters of a kilometre south along the service road, turn east at the first turn-off you find and after a further bend in the road you will be able to see, a bit further along, the track to Hazel Falls, which will be described in the next section.

17. Mabel Falls Reserve

Between Woodford and Hazelbrook, on the north side, there is a large area of bushland which is not included in the Blue Mountains National Park, but which provides some interesting walks. The area can be reached through a combination of fire trails and foot-tracks, and features several waterfalls in a network of creeks. One easy starting point is to be found at the corner of Werona Avenue and Woodbury Street, about one and a half kilometres west of Woodford Station. At the intersection of Weroona and Woodbury, you will see a fire trail going north, which is not to be confused with the dirt road to the west. The fire trail is shown on the Katoomba map, but depicted as a foot-track. Follow it north, ignoring homes and driveways on your left, and after five or ten minutes' walk through dry schlerophyll forest you will come to a large intersection where another fire trail branches off to the east. To see Mabel Falls, continue north and the trail gradually goes downhill, becoming fairly eroded and rocky.

After another five or ten minutes, the trail bends around to the west and narrows down to a foot-track as it approaches Mabel Falls. The track is getting slightly overgrown but is still quite usable; you might like to snap off the odd branch as you go through, to help keep the track clear. Not far along, you come to the east side of Mabel Falls, at a small clearing with the remains of a fire-place. At the end of a track, you look down on a circular pool dominated by the falls as they stream over a large, fern-bedecked rock shelf. The pool and waterfall are set among rich bush with fern and fern trees, making a beautiful spot which is probably the best place along this walk. If you follow the short, scrappy track down to the edge of the pool, you will see a bit of old stonework that gives the impression that the place was once a bit more developed than it is now. Looking downstream of the falls, among the scattered pieces of stonework, there is the opening of a track that leads to a picnic area on the west side of Edith Falls, which will be described later. This track is getting overgrown and is strictly for the more adventurous; it is hard to find at Mabel Falls but is clearer near the picnic area.

Going back along the original fire trail, at the bend where the fire trail turned west towards Mabel Falls, you will see a minor foot-track that goes north from the trail. This track bends around to the west, goes through a large clearing which could be used for camping, and then turns north again to go under the power-lines that cross east-west above the gully. When I went through here the track was flooded, so I did not try to go further than the power-lines and do not know just how far the track goes or exactly where it ends up. Possibly it joins the Mabel Falls creek further downstream.

Following the fire trail back to the intersection mentioned in the first paragraph, turn east and follow this trail downhill. This trail is quite badly eroded in some places, especially further along. Animal tracks make it obvious that these trails are used by both horses and cattle, which may have contributed to the wear and tear. After going downhill for a while, the trail levels off and proceeds north along the foot of a ridge, with some interesting rock formations lining the trail here and there. You soon pass under the power-lines mentioned above, and a few minutes later you come to a large intersection where the trail joins a service road that comes down from the ridge to the east. I should mention that this stretch of the trail, before the intersection, is very badly eroded, with virtual trenches having been created by the collapse of the soil, but there are minor tracks that go around the worst spots.

At the intersection of the trail and service road you will find a picnic area with a couple of fire-places and a water-tank with no tap. There are also toilets in the scrub at the north end of the picnic area. At the north-west corner you will see a track going north; not far along it, a foot-track branches off to the left and crosses the creek from Mabel Falls. A couple of logs are placed side-by-side across the creek to make crossing easier. (The original track from the north-west corner of the picnic area continues north along the edge of the gully of this creek, overlooking Edith Falls. Further down, the track bends to the east; at this point, a minor track does down the slope to the edge of the creek, some distance downstream of the waterfall. The main track, after turning east, goes back in a loop and joins the service road up to the ridge.)

After crossing the creek on the two logs, you go through a short stretch of track and emerge at the picnic area (mentioned previously) on the west side of Edith Falls. This picnic area is quite large and has a few fire-places plus some benches, although the tables have disappeared. This kind of neglect is typical of the facilities in this area, unfortunately.

Just north of the opening where the track reaches this picnic area, you will see two scribbly gums; the track continues between these two trees (the service road from the ridge passes this picnic ground on the west side, and on the other side of the service road is the track to Mabel Falls). Not far along the track, there is a rocky stretch where a turn-off goes to the right at a sharp angle. This goes down to the base of Edith Falls, and is fairly steep and eroded. The average fit person would have no trouble with it, although it is not for the aged or infirm. At the bottom of the track there is another fire-place, but not much by way of wood. Back up at the rocky stretch above, continue north for Hazel Falls. The track goes down the slope a little and then bears around towards Hazel Falls; it is getting a little overgrown these days, but is still reasonable. It bears gradually west through dry eucalypt woods overlooking a gully, and with a couple of wooden footbridges placed at strategic spots. As it approaches Hazel Falls, you will see that one branch goes up the slope to the road above while another goes directly to the falls. This latter branch goes right under the falls, taking you beneath the rock shelter that the falls plunge over.

From the falls, follow the branch up to the road above; along the way, you will pass a long rock shelter that can come in handy in a storm. Up at the road, there is no sign-post for the benefit of anyone wanting to start the walk at this end. You simply have to look for a track branching off the side of the road, with a few stone steps going down; the track is conspicuous enough. This road branches out in a few directions, and can be followed to Clear View Parade, Hazelbrook. Alternatively, follow it east to where it passes the picnic area near Edith Falls, then up onto the ridge and back to Woodford. The latter might be the best idea, since the Hazelbrook exit soon gets into suburbia, whereas the walk back to Woodford is more of a bush walk.

From the picnic areas near Edith Falls, the service road goes north-east and then south-east up the ridge. Where it is joined by the track on the east side of Edith Falls, there is yet another fire-place, plus a dead-end turn-off to the east. On top of the ridge, the service road joins Wellesley Road, which goes south to Woodford Avenue. Along this ridge there are a few Electricity Commission service roads which could offer a few more nooks and crannies for some people to explore. The walk along Wellesley Road is a pleasant ridge walk with views across the hills to the west; you may get to see the sun go down if you do the walk in the afternoon. A ridge walk like this provides a good contrast with the tracks and waterfalls down in the gullies, and is a good way to round off the walk. An average walker could complete this circuit in three or four hours without much exertion, from Woodford Station to Mabel Falls, Edith Falls, Hazel Falls and back again. For anyone wanting refreshments, there is a general store not far west of Woodford Station. The walk is, on the whole, an easy and pleasant one, with Mabel Falls probably being the most beautiful spot.

2.   Jamison Valley

The Jamison is the main valley of the Blue Mountains National Park and has much to offer walkers of all levels of fitness and experience. The north escarpment is not only the home of the famous Three Sisters, but also the starting point for a network of tracks that make it possible to do some extensive and spectacular walks. A cliff track extends all the way from the south end of Leura to the vicinity of the Scenic Skyway, providing spectacular views of the whole valley, featuring Mt Solitary and the rugged ranges south of Coxs River. Offshoots go down to the beautiful Federal Pass, which winds along the foot of the cliffs, passing through some magnificent rainforest before reaching the lower slopes of Mt Solitary. The Scenic Railway provides an easy way out for those who lack the energy for an uphill climb out of the valley.

Mt Solitary itself is traversed by an old track which would mostly appeal to bushwalkers with some experience. The mountain provides campers with the opportunity to spend a night or two in a little world that they will probably have to themselves, and a rough track down the eastern slopes makes it possible to link up with service roads through other parts of the valley. A rocky walk up Jamison Creek, or down the track from Wentworth Falls, opens up the world of the Valley of the Waters, a secluded haven in the north-east corner of the Jamison Valley and a perfect place to spend a night for those seeking complete isolation from the city.

1.   The Valley of the Waters

Tucked away in the north-east corner of the Jamison Valley, the Valley of the Waters is one of those places that make you want to keep them a secret and protect them. Its features and delights include myriad waterfalls, spectacular sandstone cliffs and the dramatic but by no means difficult National Pass. There are two main ways of entering the valley, and it would be possible to do a two-day circuit of the place that would take in virtually everything that it has to offer.

The first, and more spectacular, way to gain access is via Wentworth Falls. From the Great Western Highway, at a point just west of Wentworth Falls Station, the Falls Road goes south to end in a loop on the edge of Wentworth Falls Reserve. You will see a shelter and a foot-track directly ahead at the bottom of the road, and the track leads directly to Wentworth Falls Lookout. Paradoxically, the falls themselves cannot be seen from this

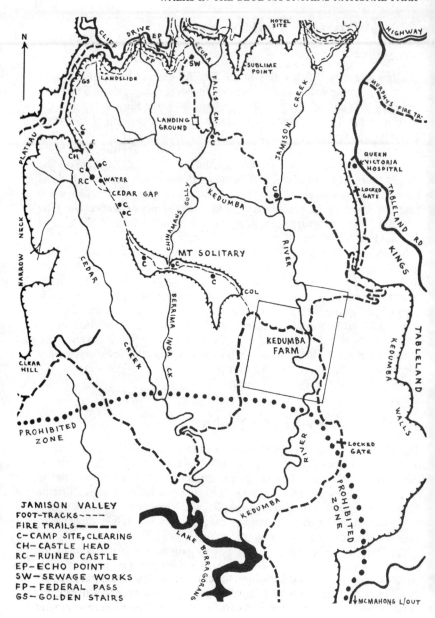

JAMISON VALLEY
FOOT-TRACKS ----
FIRE TRAILS ----
C-CAMP SITE, CLEARING
CH-CASTLE HEAD
RC-RUINED CASTLE
EP-ECHO POINT
SW-SEWAGE WORKS
FP-FEDERAL PASS
GS-GOLDEN STAIRS

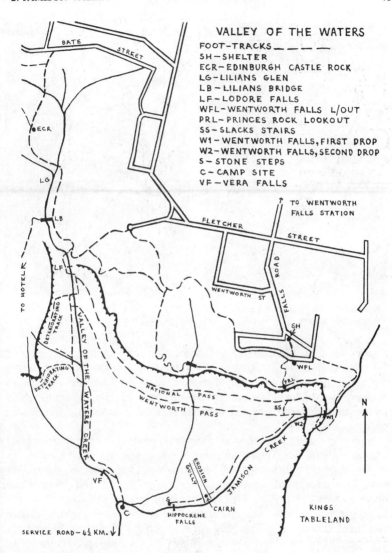

VALLEY OF THE WATERS

FOOT-TRACKS ____ _ _
SH — SHELTER
ECR — EDINBURGH CASTLE ROCK
LG — LILIANS GLEN
LB — LILIANS BRIDGE
LF — LODORE FALLS
WFL — WENTWORTH FALLS L/OUT
PRL — PRINCES ROCK LOOKOUT
SS — SLACKS STAIRS
W1 — WENTWORTH FALLS, FIRST DROP
W2 — WENTWORTH FALLS, SECOND DROP
S — STONE STEPS
C — CAMP SITE
VF — VERA FALLS

lookout, since it is too far back from the cliff, but a sign-posted track nearby leads to Princes Rock, on the edge of the cliff, where there are better views. Most photos you might see of Wentworth Falls would be taken from around here somewhere. From Princes Rock, you can follow a track east along the cliff and join the main track which crosses to the east side of Jamison

Local children at the base of Lodore Falls, Valley of the Waters

The upper drop of Wentworth Falls, showing the distinctive dome-like rock formation

Creek and then gradually winds down the cliffs to the first drop of Wentworth Falls. At the first drop you turn towards the falls themselves and go along the rocks virtually directly beneath the waterfall. This makes for some spectacular views looking up at the top of the falls, often highlighted by the sun behind or to the side of them. It can also make for a lot of spray on occasions.

Having crossed to the far side of the falls, you will pick up the National Pass straight ahead. As you go along the pass, you get some good views of the falls from a different angle, looking back towards them. Not too far along, you come to the sign-posted beginning of Slacks Stairs, which lead down to Wentworth Pass. This runs more or less parallel to the National Pass, but further down the cliff and in among the timber, giving a more cloistered kind of walk. The National Pass, on the other hand, is cut right into the cliff-face and has a very open aspect providing spectacular views of the Jamison Valley. The Wentworth Pass also provides access to an old, intermittent track that follows Jamison Creek down to its junction with the Valley of the Waters Creek. This track will be described in more detail later.

Following the National Pass, you continue around the cliff-face, gaining some breath-taking views of the valley, Kings Tableland and the towering cliff-face that hangs over you. The walk is pretty level and undemanding

The west escarpment of Kings Tableland, viewed from the National Pass

virtually all the way, and the dry, sandy nature of the setting makes quite a contrast with what you will see further down in the valley.

Eventually the track comes to the Valley of the Waters Creek and joins the main track along it, meeting it on the east side of the gully, not far below Lodore Falls (of which more later). To continue down into the valley, follow the track on the east side for a while. Before long it crosses to the west side, going a bit further downstream until it re-crosses to the east side. At the point where it first crosses to the west side of the creek, I have found that the track is a little unclear when coming back uphill on the west side. It is easy to miss the crossing and keep going up the slope on the west side, in which case you will find yourself on a minor track that bears west along the foot of the cliff; you will then have to retrace your steps to the main track by the creek. When walking downstream, however, there is no ambiguity.

While still on the west side of the creek, going downstream, you pass the sign-posted turn-off for the Wentworth Pass. A little further down, the track comes to a minor gully that joins the creek from the west side. Just before this gully there is a minor turn-off, westward, that appears to lead nowhere in particular. Ignoring this, cross the gully and continue downstream. Immediately on the south side of the gully there is another turn-off that leads west up to the foot of the cliff. This is part of a set of old tracks that follow the foot of the cliff towards Sublime Point, but which have unfortunately deteriorated and fallen into disuse. I have not personally tried to follow these tracks all the way to Sublime Point, but the more adventurous might find them interesting.

This particular turn-off is another case where there is no problem when walking downstream, but it is easy to take this turn-off accidentally when walking back up. When I went through here I put a log across the turn-off and arranged rocks to point the way along the main track, so I trust that no-one will take a wrong turn.

Further downstream, the track crosses to the east side of the creek; there is a sign-post here on the west side, but, once again, I have found that this crossing is not all that obvious when coming back up. A little scouting around would solve the problem if you found the track a little unclear on the way back up; a sign-post would also help to solve the problem. These little vague spots do not mean that this track is strictly for experienced walkers; on weekends you can see walkers of all shapes, sizes and age-groups following this track without any trouble.

Having crossed to the east side of the creek, it is only another three quarters of a kilometre down to the junction of the Valley of the Waters Creek and Jamison Creek. Along the way, you pass a turn-off to Vera Falls; an old sign-post, attached to a tree, points the way. Vera Falls are worth a detour to have a look, and make a good spot to have a break. After that, follow the track down to the junction of the two creeks. Where you reach the junction, there is a small space at the end of the track where it would be possible to put up a tent, but there is a better space on the other side of Jamison Creek. Cross Jamison Creek on the rocks, and on the south side, in a corner formed by a bend in the creek, there is a decent space for camping. This makes a good spot to spend a night, and one of those places where you feel pleasantly cut off from civilisation. It was while

Cascades along Jamison Creek, the Valley of the Waters

spending a night at this spot that I realised that, in spite of all the development that has taken place in the Blue Mountains, the character of wilderness — ie the sense of being completely cut off from civilisation — can still be experienced in no uncertain way. The Jamison Valley is a good place to go for this purpose, if you are prepared to leave the main tracks behind.

From the junction of the creeks, there is no track going further downstream, but it is of course possible to follow Jamison Creek further to where it is forded by the service trail that goes from Kings Tableland to the sewer works in the valley. You can keep going further, towards Kedumba Farm, if you are energetic enough, criss-crossing the creek where necessary. There are occasionally places where you are blocked by scrub or sheer walls, but it is always possible to cross to the other side and continue. The going is not especially difficult, although it can be tiring in the long run because of the constant clambering on rocks. The undergrowth makes it impossible to simply walk on the banks, so that it is necessary to walk on the rocks nearly all the time.

I previously mentioned an intermittent track from the Wentworth Pass to the junction of the two creeks. I was unable to find any trace of this track at the junction, but picked it up in the vicinity of Hippocrene Falls (which are not shown on the Katoomba topographic map). If you follow Jamison Creek upstream from the junction, you will find the track on your left side (ie north) as you stand facing the falls, where you will also find an excellent pool for swimming. On the slope to your left, there are some stone steps that are quite conspicuous; from these steps, follow the track further upstream until it peters out near the edge of an erosion gully. In the gully itself there is a small cairn that you should see, and on the other side you should find the continuation of the track. Further upstream, it gets a little vague for a while, but you should pick it up again sooner or later as long as you stay within sight of the creek. In contrast with the scrubby banks further downstream, the undergrowth is fairly thin along this section and it is not hard to walk along the slope. Eventually, assuming you have picked up the track again, you will come to the eastern end of the Wentworth Pass. A short extension goes further east and provides a good view of the lower part of Wentworth Falls, with another excellent pool which would come in handy if you were there in summer.

This track is easier to follow, I think, going downstream from the Wentworth Pass rather than up, but unfortunately this is also the case with the track down the Valley of the Waters Creek. Obviously, you cannot do both of them downstream, at least not on the one trip.

If you retrace your steps up the main track along the Valley of the Waters Creek, you pass the turn-off for the National Pass and continue to Lodore Falls (I might add that the Katoomba topographic map incorrectly shows this track staying on the west side of the creek all the way up to Lodore Falls, and does not show the Wentworth Pass at all). Lodore Falls are located at a rather beautiful spot where the gully takes on the atmosphere of a glen. It is a popular spot on weekends, so if possible go there on a weekday. Further upstream of Lodore Falls, the track forks and you have the choice of going east, up to the cliff and back to the Wentworth Falls area via Fletcher Street, or turning west and following the track to Lilians Glen. The former is the alternative way of entering the Valley of the Waters for those who would like to start at this section instead of starting at Wentworth Falls Reserve. Lilians Glen is a pleasant enough spot, although whether it is worth a detour is a matter of conjecture. From Lilians Glen, the track crosses the Valley of the Waters Creek and goes to Bate Street via the rock formation known as Edinburgh Castle Rock.

2. Sublime Point

Just before Lilians Glen, there is a footbridge called Lilians Bridge. On the west side of the Valley of the Waters Creek, after crossing on the bridge, you will find a track that goes up to the north edge of Leura Golf Course, or what used to be Leura Golf Course — at the time of writing, it is the site of the infamous hotel being built on the edge of the Jamison Valley. How much public access will remain when the hotel is finished is not clear, but the track used to reach the edge of the golf course and from there it

Sublime Point Lookout, with Mt Solitary in the background

was possible to cross to the south side of the links and pick up a fire trail that in turn led to Sublime Point Road. The latter can be followed to Sublime Point, in any case, whether you can use the old track from Lilians Bridge or not. Sublime Point juts straight out into Jamison Valley and provides excellent, all-round views of the valley and the ranges, like the Broken Rock Range, to the south. There is a shelter and tap near the lookout, and some basic facilities

3. Cliff Walk

There is a very good track that starts from the south end of Leura and follows the northern escarpment all the way to the Scenic Skyway near the north-west corner of the valley. This track provides some easy walking and some exceptional views of the Jamison and the rugged scenery south of Coxs River; it is well worth exploring and could be broken up into smaller sections or done as one long walk by the more energetic.

Those who want to cover the whole track could start at Links Road, which branches off Gladstone Road, Leura. The track begins at the west end of Links Road and winds for about half a kilometre until it reaches the Pool of Siloam, a small pool along Gordon Creek. The pool is shown incorrectly on the new Katoomba topographic map as being about a quarter of a kilometre north of where it really is. However, the Pool of Siloam is a pleasant place with its own waterfall and makes a good place for a break. On the west side of Gordon Creek, you will see, if you go up the slope a bit, where a track continues north and another branch goes west. The north branch comes from Spencer Street, Leura, which makes another handy place to start for those who wish to forgo the quarter-kilometre stretch from Links Road. Anyone starting at Spencer Street will find that the track goes south for a short distance and comes to a dead-end at the top of a hill where you have something of a view to the south. Shortly before reaching this dead-end, you will notice a turn-off on the west side of the track. Follow this turn-off down the slope and it will lead you along Gordon Creek and down to the Pool of Siloam.

To continue along the cliff track from the pool, take the abovementioned turn-off on the west side of the pool. This turn-off goes up the slope and then about a quarter of a kilometre south-west to Gordon Falls Reserve, at the bottom of Olympian Parade, Leura. At the reserve there is a picnic ground with taps and so forth, and a turn-off that leads to a lookout providing views of Gordon Falls. It is worth going down the turn-off for a quick look at the falls, and then the track continues further west across the Buttenshaw Bridge. Naturally, there are numerous places where good views of the

Mt Solitary viewed from the Prince Henry Cliff Walk

Jamison Valley are available, featuring Mt Solitary, Kings Tableland and the rugged ranges south of Coxs River. If you know what to look for, it is possible to make out some of the features of Kanangra-Boyd National Park, like the Gangerang Range topped by Mt Cloudmaker, and the Ti-Willa Plateau.

Further along, you pass the flying fox that goes down to the road that services the sewage works — not one of the most lovely features of the Jamison Valley, and certainly clear evidence of how low the Blue Mountains have always been rated in the view of the people of New South Wales. I wonder what we would think if the Government of Arizona decided to build some sewage works in the middle of the Grand Canyon.

In the vicinity of the flying fox you will also notice a ladder that goes down to the service road, but it is adorned with a sign saying that it is out of bounds to the public. Immediately north of the flying fox, the track approaches the top end of Leura Falls Creek and you come to a footbridge. On the other side of the bridge, the track leads up to the Cliff Drive; but ignoring the bridge and bearing south along the creek — still with the track, of course — you come to Leura Cascades. At this stage, the track fords the creek and there is a turn-off on your right which leads to a spot providing an excellent view of the cascades. This is a beautiful spot that deserves a good look and makes a great subject for photography.

On the west side of Leura Falls Creek, the track leads first to a lookout (just slightly off the main track) that provides a good bird's-eye view of Leura Falls, then climbs the slope to continue along the cliff. Almost touching the Cliff Drive in places — in the vicinity of Warne Street,

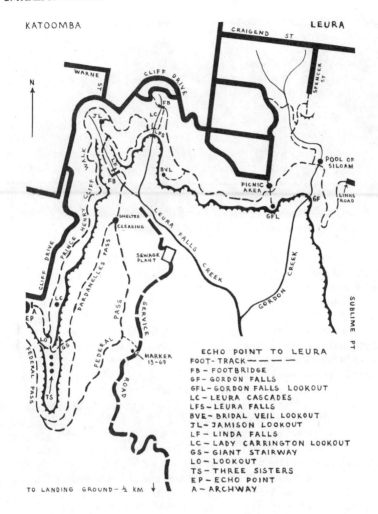

ECHO POINT TO LEURA
FOOT-TRACK — — — —
FB – FOOTBRIDGE
GF – GORDON FALLS
GFL – GORDON FALLS LOOKOUT
LC – LEURA CASCADES
LFS – LEURA FALLS
BVE – BRIDAL VEIL LOOKOUT
JL – JAMISON LOOKOUT
LF – LINDA FALLS
LC – LADY CARRINGTON LOOKOUT
GS – GIANT STAIRWAY
LO – LOOKOUT
TS – THREE SISTERS
EP – ECHO POINT
A – ARCHWAY

Katoomba — the track bypasses Jamison Lookout, which is one place to enter the Federal Pass (of which more later). In this vicinity, the track can be easily joined from the Cliff Drive.

From below the Cliff Drive, the track bends around and heads south, passing numerous lookouts, notably Lady Carrington Lookout. Photographers will find plenty to photograph around this part of the track,

Leura Cascades, a feature of the Prince Henry Cliff Walk

although they are the kind of views that can look a little washed out in the middle of the day. The late afternoon or early morning are better as far as pictures are concerned.

Just south of Lady Carrington Lookout, the track bears west and joins the track to Echo Point, the main spot for viewing the Three Sisters and, according to the tourism statistics, the most heavily visited spot in the Blue Mountains. I have nothing against the Three Sisters, but there are better views in the Blue Mountains and it is a pity that so many people think the Blue Mountains begin and end with those three hunks of rock at Echo Point.

From around the spot where the cliff track joins the track to Echo Point, there is a turn-off that goes a short distance south to a lookout where you have a fairly close view of the first of the Sisters. From this lookout, a track goes down the Giant Stairway and joins the Dardenelles Pass, one of the minor offshoots of the Federal Pass. On the way down the Giant Stairway, a footbridge provides access to a ledge on the first of the Three Sisters; there is a bench there so that you can tell everyone you actually sat on the Three Sisters. No further access to the Three Sisters is normally possible, and climbing is prohibited so that climbers will not kick rocks down onto hapless bushwalkers below. All this has not, however, stopped some enterprising entrepreneur from organising group excursions to the top of the Three Sisters, allowing people to pay for the privilege of having lunch on top of the most famous rocks in New South Wales.

Echo Point is equipped with a tourist information centre and various facilities like taps, benches, and so forth, in addition to the views of the Jamison Valley. Anyone who wants to call it a day will find it is about two and a half kilometres to Katoomba Station, via the main road. There is a

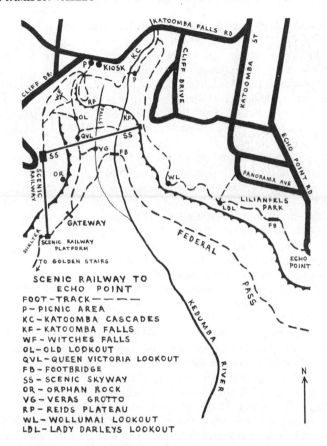

SCENIC RAILWAY TO
ECHO POINT
FOOT-TRACK — — —
P — PICNIC AREA
KC — KATOOMBA CASCADES
KF - KATOOMBA FALLS
WF - WITCHES FALLS
OL — OLD LOOKOUT
QVL — QUEEN VICTORIA LOOKOUT
FB — FOOTBRIDGE
SS — SCENIC SKYWAY
OR — ORPHAN ROCK
VG — VERAS GROTTO
RP — REIDS PLATEAU
WL — WOLLUMAI LOOKOUT
LDL — LADY DARLEYS LOOKOUT

private bus service between the station and Echo Point, but whether it will be running just when you want it is, of course, another question. Those who want to continue along the cliff track will find it on the west side of the Echo Point lookout. It is sign-posted and the first stretch of the track is covered with paving blocks, making for a very straightforward walk. The paving blocks do not last forever, of course, but the track is well graded and easy to follow. Before long you come to Lady Darleys Lookout, which can also be reached via a sign-posted track from Panorama Avenue. At the lookout there are signs pointing the way further west to the Prince Henry Cliff Walk and Katoomba Cascades.

The track continues through very dry eucalypt scrub that shows signs of being burned by wildfire, but by and large the track is in good condition and there are good views of the valley all the way along. The dominant feature is, of course, Mt Solitary, but it is also possible to make out other features like Clear Hill, Ti-Willa Plateau, Mt Cloudmaker, the Broken Rock Range and the Wanganderry Walls. The track soon leads to the Wollumi Lookout, which provides an excellent view of Mt Solitary, and then curves around to reach Katoomba Cascades after passing the cables that support the Scenic Skyway.

Katoomba Cascades are situated on the south side of the Cliff Drive and are easily reached for anyone degenerate enough to approach by car. The Prince Henry Cliff Walk reaches the east side of the Cascades and then proceeds, via a flight of steps, to a small picnic area lower down. Signposts are plentiful in this area and no-one will have any trouble following the track. From the picnic area, the track fords the creek below the cascades and works its way downstream along the gully, providing views of lower sections of the cascades. It then climbs uphill, and to the left there is a turnoff that leads to one of the many lookouts along the track, this one providing glimpses of the beautiful Katoomba Falls. After this, the track leads to an intersection consisting of cement stairs leading in various directions. One pathway leads up to the picnic area adjacent to the kiosk situated on the Cliff Drive, between Katoomba Cascades and the Scenic Railway. A second set of stairs leads up to Reids Plateau, a small outcropping where there are views of Orphan Rock and Witches Falls. The former is a rock formation jutting out alone on the edge of the valley; the latter is a small waterfall visible from the track, which does a brief loop through these places and then returns to the intersection of all the stairs. A third set of stairs leads down to the Federal Pass, with a turn-off allowing a 'round walk', as the signs say, back to the kiosk area. A further pathway is simply the return leg of the round walk. All these pathways are sign-posted and present no problems; the latter two will be dealt with in detail forthwith.

The track that goes down to the Federal Pass is more complex than the cliff walk and also steeper, although a return trip could be made via the Scenic Railway, thus eliminating any uphill clambering. From the abovementioned intersection of stairs, the track sign-posted as the one to the Federal Pass goes downhill and passes the base of Witches Falls. Going further down the slopes, the scenery changes to more of a rainforest environment that contrasts markedly with the scrub along the cliff walk, and which is quite beautiful. Below Witches Falls, the track crosses a stream by means of a footbridge; just before the footbridge, a rough branch continues down the slope into a rocky amphitheatre that is worth looking at before proceeding.

After crossing on the footbridge, the track reaches a fork where a branch goes up the slope to the Scenic Skyway; this is the round walk mentioned previously, and is sign-posted accordingly. The track going down the slope is sign-posted as the 'Federal Pass via Furber Steps', and this is the way to go for further explorations. The track was severely littered by fallen trees and branches after the storms in August 1986, but most of it was cleared quite quickly. Not far down the slope, there is an old, slightly dilapidated lookout providing good views of Katoomba Falls, showing most of the long drop down the cliff. Opposite this lookout, there is another sign-posted turn-off going up the slope, and this joins the track to the Scenic Skyway. Further down, the track comes to a level stretch with branches going east and west. The western branch is the main track to the Federal Pass, while the branch to the east goes directly to Katoomba Falls, reaching it at a point about halfway down the cliff, and thus providing an excellent view looking upwards at the top half of the falls. Photographers will appreciate this view.

Further down, the main track reaches Queen Victoria Lookout, which provides an even better view of Katoomba Falls and one of the best opportunities to appreciate their beauty. There is also a good, clear view of the Three Sisters, making this lookout very useful for the camera buffs.

From Queen Victoria Lookout, the track continues fairly steeply via steps cut into the rocks, with railings where needed. More good views of the falls are obtained further down the steps, until finally the track leads into dense forest where there is a sign-posted turn-off for Veras Grotto. This is a pleasant little hollow at the base of a small waterfall, a little to the west of Katoomba Falls. From the Veras Grotto turn-off, the main track winds its way past some interesting rock shelters and eventually goes down to the Federal Pass, joining it near the gateway near the Wildlife Sanctuary around the bottom of the Scenic Railway. According to a sign at the gateway, it is about two hundred metres to the Scenic Railway, which most people would find a convenient way to exit. Once up at the top of the Scenic Railway, it would be easy enough to pick up the Prince Henry Cliff Walk at a car park behind the administrative building near the railway, and follow the track back to the kiosk area, thus completing the round walk, or one version of it. Those who contemplate longer walks or camping trips could use the track to the Federal Pass as the starting-point for walks to the Golden Stairs, the Ruined Castle or Mt Solitary.

The round walk, of course, can also be done by picking up the abovementioned turn-off up near the old, dilapidated lookout. The turn-off zigzags up the slopes, passing a few lookouts and going through some reasonably steep sections, before reaching the gentler slopes near the top of the cliff, where there is a minor branch to the west which does a loop and rejoins the round walk a bit further below, just to keep it interesting.

This minor branch can waste a lot of energy and should be ignored. The main track proceeds through dry eucalypt forest and reaches the car park near the Skyway buildings, and at this point there is a sign saying 'Prince Henry Cliff Walk'. Whether starting at this end or at Leura, walkers will find that the cliff walk provides a beautiful walk of several kilometres, which would not be difficult for anyone even averagely fit, and which provides a striking range of views, waterfalls and beautiful forests to be enjoyed along the way.

4. Federal Pass

The Federal Pass is a major track in the Jamison that offers a great range of scenery, including waterfalls, rainforest, cliff views and some little known glimpses of the Three Sisters here and there. It is a truly magnificent track and can be joined from the Leura Falls Lookout, the Jamison Lookout or the Giant Stairway as mentioned before. From the Leura Falls Lookout, the track branches off the cliff track and goes around the slope, passing through some pleasantly forested sections liberally adorned with fern trees, before joining the track from Jamison Lookout. Where these two tracks join, there is a sign on a tree, pointing out the various ways to go; the tracks in this area are generally well sign-posted. From the sign, the track goes downhill and passes Lila Falls by means of a steel staircase — Lila Falls are actually a very minor flow of water down a rock-face, although enough to spray you a bit as you go past on the steps. A bit further along, the track turns east and crosses Leura Falls Creek on a footbridge, providing a good view of Linda Falls immediately upstream of the bridge. On the east side of the creek you may notice a minor track that leads to the sewage works, but this track is off-limits to the public. A bit further along, you pass some more waterfalls and another off-limits track to the sewage works before re-crossing to the west side of Leura Falls Creek. The Katoomba topographic map incorrectly shows this track staying on the west side of the creek all the way down, but it actually crosses and re-crosses as described above. Back on the west side, the track proceeds through pleasant, shady forest and comes to the junction with the Dardanelles Pass. This latter track is the short way to go for anyone who wants to go straight up the Giant Stairway and on to Echo Point. At the junction with the Dardanelles Pass there is a large, clear area that would make a very nice place to camp. There is also a very old, corrugated-iron shelter — a rather quaint, conically shaped creation — that might be handy sometimes, but is not guaranteed to be leak proof in a storm.

Fern trees along the Federal Pass

Some people have suggested that this stretch of the Federal Pass is a bit smelly because of the sewage plant, but I have never found it so, although I will cheer loud and long when the sewage plant finally gets up and goes elsewhere.

From the turn-off for the Dardanelles Pass, the Federal Pass begins to go downhill until it reaches a dip where the track is only a fairly short distance from the sewage plant service road. It is possible to scrub-bash from the Federal Pass to the service road, opening up the possibility of some grand tours of the valley. There is or was a faint track connecting the Federal Pass with the service road, but if you do not see it you can still work your way down. It is advisable to scout around a bit to find a way through, since the undergrowth is like a jungle in most places.

From the dip, the Federal Pass climbs uphill and gradually bears around the base of the Three Sisters until it reunites with the Dardanelles Pass just slightly to the west of the Sisters. The junction of these tracks at this point is not sign-posted and anyone coming down from the Giant Stairway would have no idea where the branch on the south side (the Federal Pass) leads if they did not have a map. Although the walks around here are mostly sign-posted, the Katoomba topographic map is still, I think, worthwhile.

The terrain along this stretch is a mixture of eucalypt and fern, and the Federal Pass continues through such scenery until coming to the shady gully of Kedumba River. The river is forded by a footbridge which provides a good vantage point for viewing Katoomba Falls, looking up at the various levels. This walk is very popular on weekends and it is advisable to go there on a weekday if possible, especially for anyone with serious photographic intentions. From Kedumba River (formerly called Kedumba Creek on the old Katoomba map, but promoted to the rank of river on the new map), a walk of about fifteen minutes will take you to the foot of the Scenic Railway, which is the short-cut up to Katoomba and the only way to leave the Federal Pass without a steep walk. Immediately west of the Scenic Railway there is a corrugated-iron shed that might be handy in a storm and, just a little further west again, a spot where there is a good view of the Three Sisters, seen in profile. Further on, you pass some old, abandoned coal mines, now barred up, and then start to bear west around Malaita Point. At this stage you are approaching the old landslide that occurred in 1931. The track up to this point is quite civilised, but around the landslide it gets messier and very rocky. It is not hard to follow, however, because there are numerous white arrows pointing the way. (You will notice, on the Katoomba topographic map, a track going from Malaita Point, down to Causeway Creek and up to the Federal Pass near the foot of the strangely named Golden Stairs. I have never noticed the entrance to this track at the Malaita Point end, but it is not too hard to find at the other end. Just south of the Golden Stairs — only a couple of minutes' walk — a narrow foot-track can be seen going down the slope at right angles to the main track. A log buttresses the edge of the main track at this point where the smaller track branches off.)

Following the white arrows from Malaita Point, pick your way around the landslide and you then get into the timber again on the west side of the landslide. Some minor watercourses around here provide water if there has been any rain. After twenty or thirty minutes you come to the Golden Stairs. I cannot say how it got its name, because it is just another foot-track. For a fit walker it is not hard to get to the top of the track in half an hour, but there is a steel ladder at one stage that makes the track unsuitable for the very young or very old. On the way up there are good views of the landslide; at the top you are on the Narrow Neck road, and from there it would be a good hour or so to walk back to Katoomba. The Golden Stairs are sign-posted at the top for the benefit of anyone starting the walk at that end.

5. Ruined Castle

From the Golden Stairs it is a superb walk down to the foot of Mt Solitary, passing through some of the most beautiful rainforest you are likely to see within easy reach of a city of three million. Before reaching Mt Solitary, of course, you pass the Ruined Castle, which is accessible via a side-track that branches off the main track to Mt Solitary. This turn-off is not sign-posted, but it has two entrances that join each other a bit further up the slope. The first entrance is the smaller one, branching off more or less at right angles to the main track and distinguished by the remains of an old water tank rusting away on the east side of the main track. A little further down is the main entrance, distinguished by a large clump of fern trees on the opposite, or east, side. Someone has arranged a line of stones pointing to the entrance to the track, but I do not know how long it will survive before the vandals have their fun with it. It is a pity that such a beautiful walk has been so neglected (it is also a pity that the National Parks and Wildlife Service insists on using wooden signs that are so easily vandalised, instead of the old iron signs like the one at the top of the Golden Stairs).

Having found either entrance to the track, follow it up the slope and then south-east along the narrow and rocky ridge to the Ruined Castle. The Castle itself is actually in several pieces. The main section is the one at the south end, and can be climbed without difficulty by working your way around the south face of the column, through a cleft between some boulders and then up and around the north face. It is not nearly as complicated as it may sound. From the top of the Castle you have good views of the whole valley, Mt Solitary, Kings Tableland and Cedar Valley. This is a great place to watch the sun come up, and certainly the best place to get shots of Mt Solitary. On the north side of the Castle, only about five minutes' walk from it, the track forks around a large boulder that provides a bit of a rock shelter on its west side; on the east side there are the remains of a camp-fire, some wood and enough space for a tent; this is a good place to spend a night for anyone who wants to make the most of the views in the morning.

From the south end of the Ruined Castle, you can keep following the track along the ridge until it rejoins the main track to Mt Solitary, just on the north side of Cedar Gap — the gap between Ruined Castle Ridge and Mt Solitary itself. Anyone interested in camping around this area will find plenty of camp-sites. There are about eight or more between the Golden Stairs and Cedar Gap, and another four or so between Cedar Gap and the lower slopes of Solitary. Once you have started to climb the mountain, however, there is nowhere to camp until you get to the top, where it flattens out; on the way up there is nothing but rock. I should mention that the only reliable source of water along the track to Solitary is an old mine shaft on the west side of the track, somewhere before Cedar Gap. There is a home-made sign attached to a tree, but you might have to look carefully to find the shaft.

6. Mt Solitary

The track up Mt Solitary is rocky and a little vague in places, and there is some scope for a few arrows. On the whole, if you stick to the crest and do not get tempted into creeping around the north face, you will be right. On the top, the mountain flattens out and there are some open, grassy areas where it is possible to camp. There is no water, of course, at this stage. From the first hump where the mountain flattens out, you go gradually downhill, ignoring a minor turn-off to the west that goes along the west face of the mountain for a short distance. At the bottom of the slope, you come to Chinamans Gully, where there is or was a sign painted on a rock, pointing the way to water about a hundred metres downstream. If you leave the main track and follow the watercourse — or what there is of it — you may eventually find water where the stream goes over the edge of the mountain, but it is perhaps not guaranteed in a dry season.

At the gully, where the sign is or was, there is a large rock shelter known

The Ruined Castle, with Castle Head in the background

Bushwalkers on top of Mt Solitary

to the initiated as Chinamans Cave, and this is a popular spot for camping; best avoided on weekends, as is the whole area. The main track is not very clear around here, but goes directly east, curling around the end of the rock shelter and going uphill from there. As you go up, you may notice a minor track branching off on the left (or north) side, but this merely doubles back to Chinamans Gully. Somewhere along this stretch you will also find some good views of Lake Burragorang.

The track continues roughly east over another hump and comes down at a point, roughly halfway along the mountain, where you are quite close to the cliff and have some good views of the valley. It is worth leaving the track for a minute to take in the view, looking back along the craggy north face of the mountain, and with general views of the valley walls. From this point, the track follows the cliff quite closely, but unfortunately gets a bit vague in places as you go further east. There is certainly scope for a bit of upgrading around here. There is a camp-site about a kilometre east of the spot with the views, and near the camp-site the track turns sharply north up some rocks. About the only way to follow it at times is to look for spots where the rocks have been worn smooth by people's boots. At the far eastern end, which is known as the Col, the track gets quite patchy; reasonably careful navigation is required. The track proceeds down the Col, following a minor gully for a while, then crosses to the opposite side of the gully to continue along the slope. It was around here that this writer lost the track, since it gets quite vague along the slope. If you lose the track, the descent of the slopes is quite rough and slippery, but by no means impossible or dangerous if you are careful. It would be fair to say, however,

2. JAMISON VALLEY   61

that this whole section is for experienced walkers only. I understand this walk is quite popular with bushwalking clubs, in which case it would be a nice gesture if they would take some spray-paint along and mark the track for the benefit of us plebs. When I went through, there were occasional marks like cuts on branches and trees, but the track is still hard to follow and could do with more marking.

When I bumbled down the slope I tended to drift east and eventually came to Kedumba River, well north of Kedumba Farm. Continuing downstream, I came to an old jeep-track that led up to the Kedumba Valley Road, but I would not, unfortunately, be able to pin-point this jeep-track now. If you succeed in following the track down the Col, you come to the service road west of Kedumba Farm. From there you should skirt around Kedumba Farm and you then have the choice of following the road up to Kings Tableland and Wentworth Falls, or following Kedumba River upstream to the service road to the sewage plant; from these, the road could be followed east to Kings Tableland or west towards the Federal Pass. The more energetic might like to follow Jamison Creek right up to the Valley of the Waters. The possibilities are endless.

The road on the west side of Kedumba Farm offers the possibility for an interesting circuit of the southern end of the valley, linking up with the roads at Medlow Gap and then going up the Megalong Road to Blackheath or joining the Six Foot Track, which will be covered in detail in another section. The road around the south end of the Jamison is something I have never got around to, but from what I have seen of the valley it is likely that there would be some beautiful forest along the way. There is a stretch of about eight kilometres, however, where the road passes through the prohibited zone around Lake Burragorang, so the Water Board should be consulted for the latest information on permits.

7. Sewage Plant Service Road

The above title may not sound very inspiring, but the service road from the sewage plant to Kings Tableland provides the opportunity for some decent walks and extensions to camping trips that might otherwise not stray far from the well-worn tracks near the cliffs. As mentioned in Section Four, you can join the service road from the Federal Pass, and the resulting walk will take you through some beautiful forest, especially between the Federal Pass and Leura Falls Creek. A couple of kilometres along the road, you come to a helicopter landing ground which can be a reasonable place to camp and which happens to provide a good view of the Three Sisters silhouetted against the sky. Any photographers who are interested in getting shots of the Three Sisters, other than the same tired old shots from Echo Point, and who are prepared to go to some trouble, could do worse than walk down to this landing ground. A good tele lens is necessary, since the Sisters are fairly distant.

For anyone interested in going further in this direction, there is a clearing on the west side of Leura Falls Creek, where camping would be possible if you do not mind a little occasional traffic in the form of workers from the sewage plant going by in four-wheel drives. There is, however, a better spot further on. There is also a sign at Leura Falls Creek saying the water is not safe to drink. Going further west, there are more views of the Three Sisters and some good views of Sublime Point, before you reach Jamison Creek, where you will find a camp-site with a stone fire-place on the west side of the creek. There is a decent pool just a little downstream of where the road fords the creek, but as far as drinking is concerned I do not know if Jamison Creek is any safer than Leura Falls Creek. Chlorine tablets would be a good idea.

On the east side of the creek, the road passes through more pleasant forest and joins the Kedumba Valley Road, providing walking access to Kings Tableland and Wentworth Falls. There is a locked gate at the top, but workers from the sewage plant have assured me that this is only to keep traffic out; walkers are allowed. When I spent a couple of nights at the camp-site beside Jamison Creek, I found the Water Board workers very friendly as well as curious; they are used to people walking through, but no-one camps there.

For the benefit of anyone who wants to do this walk in reverse, from around Jamison Creek to the Federal Pass, a little tip is offered. All along the service road, you will see white plastic markers with numbers on them, placed at the side of the road. When you come to a marker with the numbers 13-69, you will see a minor gully that comes down from the Federal Pass. This is the best place to go up the slope to the Pass if you cannot find the faint track mentioned in Section Four; it is a bit rough, but still better than going straight through the heavy undergrowth.

8. Narrow Neck Plateau

Narrow Neck is the long, spindly peninsula that separates the Jamison from the Megalong Valley, and begins broadly on the south-west side of Katoomba. From the Cliff Drive, a road branches off and goes the entire length of the plateau, ending at Clear Hill on the southern tip of the Plateau. The first section of this road is technically known as the Glenraphael Drive, but the road in general is casually known as the Narrow Neck road, and

The west escarpment of Narrow Neck Plateau

can be found about three kilometres from Katoomba Station. The road provides spectacular views in many directions, as well as walking access to some far-flung corners of the Blue Mountains and Kanangra.

In the first kilometre of the road there are good views of the landslide at Malaita Point, making it a good place for anyone who wants to get shots of the landslide. Around this section there is also the Water Board road that goes to the west side of the plateau and provides access to ladders that go down into the Megalong Valley, as described in the following chapter. This part of the plateau provides good views of both the Megalong and Jamison Valleys.

About a kilometre past the Water Board road is the beginning of the Golden Stairs, which is marked with a good, old-fashioned iron sign that has stood the test of time and vandals for many years. This is a good place to start walks to Mt Solitary, the Ruined Castle or any of the exits along the Federal Pass in the direction of Katoomba or Leura. About two kilometres further south of the Golden Stairs, there are minor tracks on the east side of the road, leading to the Castle Cliff Trig on Castle Head — another good place to look at the views, but the topographic maps of Katoomba and Jamison would be worth having for anyone interested in these tracks. I should mention that the road is quite rough around here and is mostly suitable for four-wheel drives, although I have seen some people go down in camper vans.

About two kilometres further south of the Castle Head tracks, the road goes downhill and then onto a very narrow stretch where the plateau could not be more than fifty metres wide. This spot provides very good views of both valleys and especially of Mt Solitary, which is seen here from its western side and looks quite different from the long, sprawling shape seen from Echo Point. The two-way views could make this spot a good place to spend a night; you would get views of the sun setting over the Megalong Valley and then rising the next day over the Jamison. Go there when there is a full moon and you could watch the moon come up over the Jamison just after the sun goes down over the Megalong. There is certainly no great camp-site, but anyone who does not mind roughing it could find an adequate patch, providing they take their own water. A camper van would be an ideal way to do it.

For the next four kilometres or so, the road is fairly uneventful, although still providing views of the valleys and some glimpses of Lake Burragorang, very much in the distance. On the west side of the road there is a fire tower which is used for keeping an eye on bushfires around the Burragorang catchment area, and would provide great views if it were open to the public, which it is not. Some sections of the plateau provide access to the Megalong Valley via some obscure passes known mostly to experienced bushwalkers and suitable only for experienced bushwalkers; I personally have not investigated them, but anyone who is interested should acquire the Dunphy sketch map 'Gangerang' from places like Paddy Pallins, and preferably contact experienced walkers through bushwalking clubs.

From the fire tower, it is about three kilometres to Clear Hill, a partly timbered knoll that stands at the end of the plateau and provides views in all directions. There is no camp-site but, once again, anyone who likes to rough it could find this a rewarding place to spend a night. The views extend all over the Jamison Valley, the Megalong Valley, Lake Burragorang, the Wild Dog Mountains, the Gangerang Range and the Ti-Willa Plateau. If you know where to look, it is even possible to dimly make out the shape of Kanangra Walls. Clear Hill, conversely, can be seen from Kanangra, Leura, McMahons Lookout, Sublime Point and God knows how many other distant places. You could hardly ask for a better place to enjoy early-morning views (there is no water, of course).

Where the road comes to Clear Hill, you will see a track on the west side, branching off roughly at forty-five degrees. This is the track to Little Cedar Gap, Mt Debert and Medlow Gap. The track goes through a narrow cleft between sandstone walls and then continues south around the bottom slopes of Clear Hill, at one stage reaching a steep section where the only access is via steel spikes known as Taro's Ladder. At the top of the ladder there is a plaque with the following dedication:

In memory of Our Beloved Bushwalker Taro
"The Duke of Clear Hill"
For whom the sun set August 14, 1969
Walter Taro
Aged 90 Years

The spiked ladder is not hard to get up or down, but for those going down there is a bit of a jump at the bottom, making it necessary to be careful, especially if carrying a backpack. After the ladder, the track proceeds straightforwardly enough to Cedar Gap — the gap between Narrow Neck and Mt Debert. At Cedar Gap there is an electricity tower supporting power-lines that go right across the Jamison and Megalong Valleys — these are the same lines that are encountered at the Blue Drum Waterhole on Kings Tableland. From the tower at Cedar Gap, a service road can be seen on the east side, and this provides access to the service roads that go around the south end of the Jamison, as mentioned in Section Six. Alternatively, walkers can proceed along a track south of the electricity tower; this track goes over Mt Debert and down to Medlow Gap, the gap between Mt Debert and the Wild Dog Mountains. Medlow Gap will be treated in the next chapter.

3. Megalong Valley

The Megalong Valley, west of the Jamison, has been settled since the early days of the 19th century, after the botanist Thomas Jones followed Coxs River as far as the present site of Hartley. After his expedition, cattlemen used the valley and the area around Coxs River for grazing, while settlers travelled through the area on their way west from Camden. In the 1880s, a trail was blazed from Nellies Glen, in the east escarpment of the valley, to Jenolan Caves, opening up an alternative route to Jenolan that became known as the Six Foot Track. A shale mine also operated in the Megalong at around the same time and became the focal-point for a small village which eventually died when the mine closed down. Access to the valley was improved by the construction of a road through Blackheath Glen, by which time the valley was well established as a farming area.

Today most of the Megalong is still in private hands and only the southern part is in the national park, but bushwalkers and other visitors can still find plenty of room to move. The east escarpment contains a number of lookouts that provide excellent views of the valley, and walking tracks descend to the valley floor from Nellies Glen, the Devils Hole and spots outside Blackheath. The Water Board's steel ladders on the Narrow Neck Plateau also provide access to the roads and trails in the Megalong, while Medlow Gap is the centre of a whole network of tracks that radiate like the spokes of a wheel. These tracks open up the beautiful country of Coxs River and the more challenging ranges of Kanangra-Boyd National Park, where experienced walkers can seek refuge for days on end.

1. The Devils Hole, Boars Head Rock

On the south-west edge of Katoomba, the escarpment of the Megalong Valley creates a number of features in its outcroppings and recesses. Two of the most notable features are Boars Head Rock and the appropriately named Devils Hole. Both are reached via the Cliff Drive, where it bends west from Narrow Neck Road, which should not be confused with the road down Narrow Neck Plateau. The Katoomba topographic map would be of assistance in this matter. Going west along the Cliff Drive, you actually come to the Devils Hole first, but let us dispose of Boars Head Rock before going down the Hole.

You will pass, first of all, a track entrance where there is a metal pole that may once have had a sign but does no longer (at the time of writing).

The main cleft of the Devils Hole   Boars Head Rock

This is the main entrance to the Devils Hole. Further up the Cliff Drive, you will pass another entrance where there are eight white posts but no sign. Further past this, where the road begins to bend right (north), a row of white marker poles begins at the side of the road, and this is where you will find the track to Boars Head Rock. The track leads down to a spot from which you have a good view of the Megalong Valley with the rock in the foreground. From this spot you are looking at the rear of the rock and cannot see the distinctive boar's-head shape, which is quite striking. To see this, you must move further around the cliff to the north of the rock to obtain a view of it in profile. There is a rough track along the cliff, but retrace your steps carefully because the tracks are a little vague around here. The Boars Head Rock can also be viewed to advantage from the road down the Narrow Neck Plateau, or more specifically from the Water Board service road that leads to the ladders mentioned in the previous chapter. From that area you have a good view of the rock in profile, although it is rather distant.

To get to the Devils Hole, go down the track where you see the metal pole minus sign. The other track, where the eight white posts are, may or may not be the secondary entrance to the Devils Hole, as shown on the Katoomba topographic map, but it has so many forks, without signs or markers, that it is best left alone. The main track into the Devils Hole starts off well enough, being a little rocky but still quite reasonable. As it descends, you come into the main part of the Devils Hole, a narrow pass down through the cliffs. As the Hole starts to tower above you, it takes on quite a spectacular appearance, all the more so because of the huge boulder jammed high up in the crevice. Looking up at it, you cannot help hoping that the boulder will not come loose one day and descend on someone.

The track through the main crevice is rocky but reasonable, although it is worth taking some care, especially if you are carrying the weight of a backpack. Below the crevice, however, the track becomes progressively more vague. There are red metal markers here and there which are of some help, but as the track gets vaguer the markers start to disappear. Eventually the track disappears completely and so do the markers, a state of affairs that elicited some rich purple prose from this writer until the nature of the problem was realised.

You will see, on the Katoomba map, that the track starts on the east side of the watercourse that flows through the Devils Hole, then crosses to the west side before finally re-crossing to the other side much further down. It happens that the track is virtually non-existent by the time it crosses the stream from east to west, and if you are still following it at all it is only by looking for tell-tale signs like rocks that have been worn smooth by many walking shoes. The track virtually disappears for what must be close to a kilometre, and the only thing to do is to keep bearing broadly west and down the slope until, if you are lucky, you will stumble onto the track again lower down, where it reappears on its way to the service road at the bottom of the steel ladders. The track then re-crosses the abovementioned watercourse, which is by now known as Devils Hole Creek, and joins the service road at a spot that is marked by a small cairn and a red marker on a tree.

Until this track is upgraded or at least properly marked, I cannot recommend it except to experienced walkers who will not panic when the track disappears. The track vanishes in an environment that is not unlike a jungle, and it is a hell of a place for beginners to lose a track. My first reaction was to think that the people responsible for marking this track should be strung up, but then I realised that the problem was that the people trying to mark the track obviously could not follow it themselves, which is why they could not mark it. I presume the local council is responsible for maintaining these tracks, and until something is done the Devils Hole must be considered for experienced walkers only. Of course, anyone who wants to have a look at it could always do a shortened walk by following the track until it starts to disappear, then turning around and going back.

Anyone who follows the track all the way to the service road below could return via Nellies Glen, which is about four kilometres from the junction of the Devils Hole track and the service road. It would simply be a matter of going west for one kilometre and then turning up the Nellies Glen Road, all of which is shown on the Katoomba map. Alternatively, walkers could turn east and follow the service road to the vicinity of the steel ladders, where there are a couple of signs in silver spray paint to point the way. The ladders ascend the cliff — which is the west escarpment of the Narrow Neck Plateau — in a few stages; they are enclosed by a wire cage most of the way and are quite easy to climb, except presumably for the aged, infirm or small children. At the top, a track leads to the service road that joins the Narrow Neck fire trail, with some more silver arrows along the way. I do not know what the Water Board's official policy is on people using these ladders, but so many people do it that there is not likely to be any problem.

A long-winded alternative for anyone who goes down the Devils Hole would be to follow Nellies Glen Road down to Megalong Road and then follow the latter all the way to Blackheath. This would add an extra sixteen kilometres or so to the walk and would obviously be suited only to fit walkers, who could do it if they gave themselves plenty of walking time.

2. The Six Foot Track

The Six Foot Track was originally developed in the 19th century as a bridle trail from Katoomba to Jenolan. This became a popular way of making the journey to Jenolan Caves, but eventually fell into disuse as the car became more widely used and road access improved. Parts of the track were absorbed into private property and other parts were overtaken by roads and fire trails, making it a dubious proposition for anyone interested in walking from Katoomba to Jenolan. However, in recent years the track has been upgraded by the Crown Lands Office working together with the Jenolan Caves management and the Blue Mountains City Council. The track has been well sign-posted and legal access has been arranged with property owners where necessary, so there is no longer any problem in using the track for what can be a three-day walk, although parts of it can be sub-divided into shorter walks. A pamphlet on this walk can be obtained free of charge from the Department of Lands, Bridge Street, Sydney, and is worth having for anyone who is interested in the walk.

The track officially begins at the Explorers Tree, on the edge of the Great Western Highway, two kilometres west of Katoomba Station. This tree was marked by Blaxland, Lawson and Wentworth when they crossed the Blue Mountains, and is now preserved as a historic monument. It has been filled

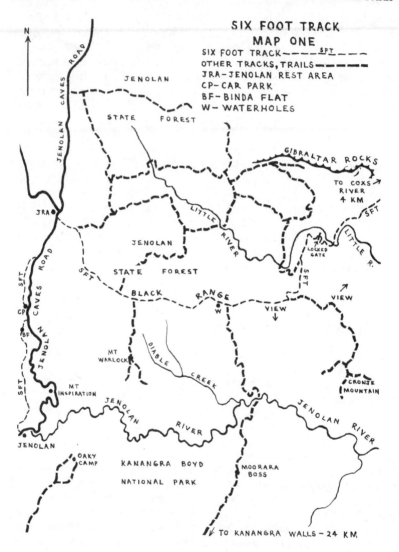

with cement to make it keep its shape, and covered with a protective roof that makes it look, from a distance, like a rather quaint out-house. From the Explorers Tree, there is a track that goes north and leads up to the top of Pulpit Hill, where there are a number of graves which are the burial places of convicts who worked on the Bathurst Road. They can be seen

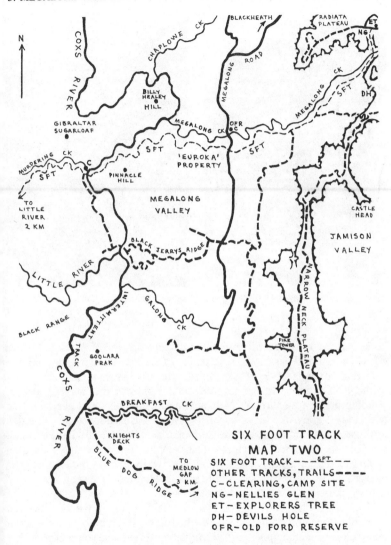

SIX FOOT TRACK
MAP TWO
SIX FOOT TRACK――-SFT――
OTHER TRACKS, TRAILS----
C―CLEARING, CAMP SITE
NG―NELLIES GLEN
ET―EXPLORERS TREE
DH―DEVILS HOLE
OFR―OLD FORD RESERVE

in a clearing on top of the hill, and consist of low mounds with rough headstones. This track is not part of the Six Foot Track itself, but the convict graves are of some interest.

From the Explorers Tree, Explorers Road proceeds west and you will see signs showing where the track turns off and goes south to Nellies Glen,

The Explorers Tree, where the Six Foot Track begins

Nellies Glen, unfortunately marred by the attempt to build a fire trail through it, but steadily recovering

initially in the form of a fire trail until you get to the top of the glen. Nellies Glen is a beautiful pass in the escarpment of the Megalong Valley, and was named after the daughter of J.B. North, who ran a shale mine in the valley in the 19th century. In the seventies, someone had the inspired idea of building a fire trail through Nellies Glen to provide rapid access to the Megalong Valley in case of bushfires. Spoil was bulldozed into the glen to provide a foundation, but the attempt was unsuccessful and the result was, of course, to detract from the beauty of the glen. Nowadays, the glen is recovering as some of the spoil gets washed away and some gets overgrown, and it is still beautiful in spite of humanity's best efforts to ruin it.

Parts of the original Six Foot Track are still visible in the glen, as well as an old stone culvert to one side of the track. At the bottom of the glen, the track crosses the upper part of Megalong Creek and you will probably notice the sound of the nearby Bonnie Doon Falls. There is no track as such to the falls, but it is not difficult to clamber over the rocks and through the scrub to get a view of the waterfall before continuing with the walk. From Megalong Creek, the track continues another kilometre or so through quite pleasant forest before joining Nellies Glen Road, which proceeds westward through some properties where legal access has been arranged.

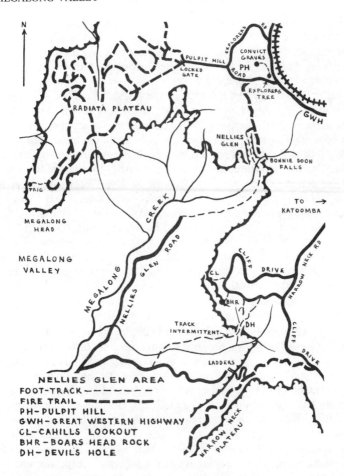

In some places there are stiles to allow walkers to get over fences, and there are always enough signs or red markers to show the way. Approaching the Megalong Road, the track leaves Nellies Glen Road and heads across farmland to arrive at Megalong Road about a third of a kilometre south of the Old Ford Reserve. The latter reserve is situated where the Megalong Road crosses Megalong Creek, and can be used for camping.

On the west side of Megalong Road, the track continues directly opposite, passing through the 'Euroka' property; as a sign explains, access has been arranged by courtesy of the property owners and walkers are asked to keep to the marked track and respect the property. Please note that there is nowhere to camp between Megalong Road and Coxs River. For about the first two kilometres west of Megalong Road, the track consists of a farm access road and there is some very nice scenery along the way, featuring the hills and fields of the valley plus the cliffs of the Narrow Neck Plateau and Shipley Plateau to the north.

After the first couple of kilometres, the original Six Foot Track comes into its own and is marked with the usual red markers as well as some home-made white markers, consisting of the circular tops of kerosene drums that have been painted white and nailed to trees along the track. These are a useful guide if you do not see red markers at every turn, but by and large you will have no trouble following the track. After leaving the farm access road behind, the track proceeds through eucalypt forest for about four kilometres before reaching a spot where it fords Coxs River. There are conspicuous sign-posts around this spot; the river is narrow and rocky and is quite easy to cross unless it is flooded, which would not be too often. On the west side of the river there is a spacious camp ground with fire-places and a toilet. Firewood is not plentiful but can be found if you look around; as the track becomes more popular, firewood could become a problem around this section.

On the south-west side of the camp ground you will see the access road that continues west for the next stage of the walk. For the next three kilometres or so, you have quite a solid uphill walk to get out of the river area. For most of the way, the road follows the gully of Murdering Creek, which was quite dry when I went through. Around the top of the rise, you pass some yards and possibly some sheep and cattle, and anywhere around here you could be blessed by the company of trail bikes, which unfortunately have not been locked out of the area. There is a locked gate further on, past Little River, but for some reason they left room for trail bikes to get around.

From around the Mini Mini Saddle, which is about four kilometres west of Coxs River and shown on the Jenolan topographic map, the road starts to go downhill towards Little River, making a nice change after the uphill stretch. As you come to Little River, there are some very pleasant, green sections with pines and willows, although there are also some dense, thorny bushes along the river to keep us in our place.

The road soon fords Little River, which does not come from any built-up areas and should, presumably, be safe for drinking whenever it is flowing. The pamphlet put out by the Department of Lands suggests 'carrying drinking water'; I presume they do not seriously expect people to carry a three-day supply of water, and it is, of course, not necessary. There are adequate supplies of water along the way.

Further west of Little River, the road begins the steep ascent of the Black

Megalong Creek, not far from the Six Foot Track

The Megalong Valley seen from the Six Foot Track, looking towards Shipley Plateau

Range, and this is another very solid uphill walk for about three kilometres. As you get near the top, there is a good view back across the Megalong Valley, and this is also the case along the uphill stretch out of Coxs River. At the top of the Black Range you come to the fire trail that goes east-west along the range, from Cronje Mountain to Jenolan Caves Road. When you reach the top you will be glad of a rest if you walked non-stop from Little River — this is the kind of place where you want a porter to carry your pack.

Proceeding west along Black Range, you may notice glimpses of the Gangerang Range and Mt Cloudmaker to the south, between the trees. About two kilometres along, you come to the turn-off that goes south to the Jenolan River (this fire trail continues all the way to Kanangra Walls Road and presents the possibility of an interesting walk from Katoomba to Kanangra). Immediately west of this trail, there are two waterholes on the south side of the Black Range trail — these waterholes are not mentioned on the Six Foot Track pamphlet or shown on the topographic map, but they are potentially very handy. The walk from Coxs River to Jenolan Caves Road is a very solid one that took me about seven and a half hours; if it looks like you might not make it before dark, you could take water from one of these holes and camp somewhere along the Black Range. The water, is, of course, stagnant but can be chlorinated. The more westerly of the holes looked the deeper of the two, the other being quite shallow at the time I saw it.

The forest along the Black Range is, of course, dry eucalypt, with some fascinatingly gnarled old trees to admire along the way. The trail undulates mildly and is basically undemanding. Eventually you come to the pine plantations around the east side of the Jenolan Caves Road; camping is, as the pamphlet points out, not allowed in pine plantations, but along the rest of the Black Range the undergrowth is quite thin and it would not be hard to find places to camp if necessary.

On the west side of the Jenolan Caves Road, directly opposite the Black Range trail, is the Jenolan State Forest Rest Area, which has some basic picnic facilities and can be used for camping. Water is provided by a single tap beside a pine tree, another fact strangely omitted from the pamphlet. This is certainly a pleasant spot, especially with all the pine trees around, but unfortunately camping here means getting the noise of traffic and trail bikes. Personally, I camped about ten minutes' walk from the road, in the scrub on the south side of the Black Range trail, and I was no doubt better off there. The only real advantage of the rest area is the tap.

From the rest area you begin the final leg of the walk, a nine-kilometre stretch that is largely downhill. For about the first three kilometres it is unfortunately necessary to walk along the Jenolan Caves Road, but around the three-kilometre mark there is a fire trail on the west side. This is blocked with a lot of fallen trees, but there is a red marker indicating that it is the continuation of the Six Foot Track. For some reason this fire trail has not been indicated on the pamphlet; it is only about a kilometre long, but worth following to get away from the traffic. At the south end of the trail there is a car-park and then you are back on the main road. Not far south of the car-park you will see the entrance to Binda Flats, which is an open area where cabins have been built, and bookings can be made to stay there through Caves House at Jenolan. The pamphlet says that camping is permitted at Binda Flats and there are several water taps. The trail from the main road continues south past the Flats — there are signs along the way — until you come to a barrier where there is another sign saying 'Six Foot Track'.

From the barrier, the fire trail continues for a few kilometres to Mt George, passing through some of the most pleasant country encountered on this walk. The forest is similar to that along the Black Range, but generally greener, with trees covered in moss and lichen. There are some glimpses of the Wild Dog Mountains to the east, and altogether this must be one of the best parts of the trip. For anyone who somehow managed to get stuck around here at the end of the day, there are enough spaces to allow for camping along the first kilometre south of Binda Flats, but not much after that. At Mt George, the Six Foot Track leaves the fire trail and bears south-west down the slopes towards Jenolan. This is part of the original Six Foot Track, and when you see the slopes you will be glad you are going downhill rather than up.

Further down, the track passes the distinctive Carlotta Arch, with a view of the Blue Lake — formed by putting a weir across the Jenolan River — framed by the arch. The track then zigzags further down, giving good views of Jenolan and Caves House, and finally emerges directly opposite Caves House, where it is conspicuously sign-posted for the benefit of anyone starting the walk at this end. While at Jenolan, it is worth doing some guided tours of some of the caves, which are a real wonderland. There is a restaurant and kiosk at Jenolan if anyone wants refreshments when they get there; on long weekends, the queue at the kiosk can be about half a mile long.

This completes a walk of about forty-two kilometres, or forty-four from Katoomba Station. The walk can, of course, be done the other way around, but my impression is that it would be easier from Katoomba. From Katoomba to Jenolan, there are only two main uphill sections: west of Coxs River and west of Little River. From Jenolan, however, there are four uphill sections: north out of Jenolan, east from Little River, east from Coxs River and, of course, Nellies Glen. Whichever way you do the walk, you may want to make use of the coach that goes from Katoomba to Jenolan and back again a few times a week. This is run by Golden West Tours of

Carlotta Arch, Jenolan, viewed from the Blue Lake. The Six Foot Track passes the arch, providing a view of the lake framed by it

Caves House, Jenolan, where the Six Foot Track comes to an end

Katoomba, who can be contacted on 047 821866. The Six Foot Track offers a varied three-day walk which is marred only by trail bikes and the traffic on Jenolan Caves Road. How significant this is depends on how sensitive you are to noise; for anyone who particularly dislikes the racket made by trail bikes, this is definitely a walk to be done on weekdays if it can be arranged.

3. Black Range Track

Anyone familiar with Miles Dunphy's sketch map 'Gangerang' may be aware of a 'track' that goes from the eastern end of the Black Range trail down to the junction of Little River and Coxs River. This presents an interesting alternative to the main Six Foot Track for part of its length, although it is for experienced walkers only. The track is, in fact, now virtually non-existent, which some people might like to know in case they had ideas of using it.

The beginning of what used to be this track is marked by conspicuous blazes on a couple of trees beside the Black Range trail, precisely where they should be at 353574 on the Jenolan topographic map. You should have no trouble finding the blazes, but from that point there is no track and you have to navigate through the forest, first east and then north-east, to follow the ridge down to the junction of the two rivers. After about two kilometres you should come to a kind of rocky knoll from which there are good views of the Wild Dog Mountains and Megalong Valley; you can see Coxs River and the road up Black Jerrys Ridge. Below this knoll, the slopes get very steep and slippery, the kind of place where it is worth dragging your pack behind you to make sure you do not slide willy-nilly down the slope. In my case, I took a detour near Slaughterhouse Gully, which is steep but not as grim as the name implies, and then walked up Coxs River.

It would be nice if this track still existed, but there is nothing but old animal tracks which are not always of much help. Since the slopes are so steep, it is naturally easier to go down this one rather than up. It could be useful for anyone interested in walks along the Black Range, from west to east. I mention it not so much for the sake of recommending it as for the sake of pointing out that the track is no longer there; the ridge, nevertheless, could be handy in spite of the demise of the track, but it is strictly for experienced walkers who are good at navigation.

4. Medlow Gap

Medlow Gap is something of a waystation for walkers, providing access in a number of directions. To the south-east there are the roads to the southern parts of the Jamison, passing partly through the prohibited zone, as said in the Jamison chapter. To the north there is the road to the Megalong Valley and the Six Foot Track, opening up a few possibilities for round trips. The Six Foot Track would be about fourteen kilometres north of Medlow Gap, with about half of this being through the Blue Mountains National Park and the rest through the partly cleared land of the Megalong. It would be about thirty-two kilometres from Medlow Gap to Blackheath, about two days' walk for an averagely fit walker with backpack.

To the west there is the service road to Kelpie Point on Coxs River, which in turn opens up more walking possibilities, like the track up to Scotts Main Range, which will be treated more fully in Chapter Six. Coxs River itself offers considerable scope for walks; walkers could do no better than a trip from Kelpie Point to the Six Foot Track (or vice versa), following the river all the way. The scenery along Coxs River is very beautiful and would provide a great walk for a couple of days or so, walking sometimes along the banks and sometimes on rocks. I should point out that, because of the

large number of farms upstream, the water is not considered terribly safe
to drink and should be boiled or chlorinated — a piece of advice that should
be noted by anyone contemplating the walk along the Six Foot Track.

The road from Medlow Gap to Kelpie Point also provides walking access
to the Wild Dog Mountains and thence to Kanangra via Yellow Pup Point
and Mt Strongleg — all of which is strictly for experienced walkers, of
course, who could probably make use of the 'Gangerang' map (which I
do not, unfortunately, get a commission for plugging). There is also a track
from the Wild Dog Mountains to the junction of Breakfast Creek and Coxs
River, from where more walks can be done in a couple of directions. The
Jenolan topographic map is necessary for venturing into this area, which
should be regarded as suitable only for experienced walkers or those
accompanied by them. A few years ago, a couple of walkers went for a
walk around Breakfast Creek, took a wrong turn and were eventually found
somewhere near Jenolan, after a search that lasted two or three days. I was
told that the man was wearing shorts in spite of the fact that it was winter.
This area certainly provides some interesting possibilities, but walkers should
realise the demanding nature of the terrain and make sure they are well
equipped and well prepared.

Medlow Gap itself is the site of a large clearing that is used as a helicopter
landing ground, as well as being used by bushwalkers for camping. There
is plenty of room for everyone, although naturally it is a good idea not to
camp right in the middle of the clearing in case a helicopter came down
on top of one's tent. There is a small waterhole that comes in very handy
if the water is boiled or chlorinated, obviating the need for anyone to carry
water all day if they are heading for Medlow Gap.

5. Radiata Plateau

Radiata Plateau juts like a large proboscis into the Megalong Valley just
west of the Katoomba area, and provides some scope for simple day-walks.
The plateau is the site of a pine plantation from which the name is derived,
and walkers should naturally take heed of the usual restrictions that go with
such plantations, ie no camping, no fires and no damage to the trees. The
pines can provide quite a pleasant environment for walking, and the plateau
is also used by locals for horse riding. Entrance is gained via Pulpit Hill
Road, where the Explorers Tree is found, or via Explorers Road on the
north side of Pulpit Hill.

About a kilometre down Pulpit Hill Road you will come to a locked gate
which marks the entrance to the pine plantation. On the other side of the
gate, the service road continues along the south-east side of the plantation,

which means that you have pines on one side and eucalypt forest, with glimpses of the Megalong Valley, on the other. About two kilometres down the road, you come to a rough clearing, on the other side of which the road continues in the form of a very scrappy jeep track. This jeep track bends around to the north and before long you will see, on the west side, the remains of a camp fire, which should not be used. Not far past the camp fire, you should see, also on the west side, two small cairns which mark the beginning of a track that goes to the trig on Megalong Head. The track is not the best in the world, but can be followed without too much trouble across the rocky western slopes of Megalong Head until you come to the trig, from which there are good views to the west, across the valley, and to the south, along the escarpment of Narrow Neck and down towards the ranges of Kanangra.

Back on the jeep track again, you can follow it as it bears roughly north-east around the pine plantation, and have fun getting lost in the maze of service roads around the plateau. The Katoomba topographic map would be worth having.

4. Grose Valley

Although well known among bushwalkers, the Grose is not so familiar to the public at large and yet is probably more deserving of recognition than any other part of the Blue Mountains. It is quite arguable that, if Australia has a Grand Canyon, it is right outside Blackheath in the form of the Grose Valley. The Grose River, flowing between Bell Range and the Blue Mountains Range, has carved out a magnificent canyon of sandstone walls that taxed the energies of a number of early explorers and surveyors, like Paterson, Caley and Govett.

The ruggedness of the valley also protected it from farming, although a certain amount of coal-mining took place and still takes place at the Grose Valley Colliery near Bell. Most of the valley and its environs are, however, contained and protected by the national park, which creates the opportunity for some magnificent walks. Cliff tracks and lookouts outside Blackheath provide some of the most spectacular views in New South Wales and probably in the whole of Australia. Numerous tracks also descend to the valley floor and create the chance to do walks that take in some beautiful scenery and which can last for a few hours or a few days. The beautiful Blue Gum Forest, at the junction of the Grose River and Govetts Creek, can be reached by a number of tracks, and from there a more extended walk can be done around to Mt Victoria. Passes provide steep walking access to major features like Mt Hay and Mt Banks, while those who really like to rough it could explore the eastern half of the Grose, largely trackless and offering a winding stretch of virtual wilderness that might rival the Colo River. Much of the valley was burned out in 1982, but has regenerated well.

1. Mt Hay

Mt Hay is one of the dominant features of the south side of the Grose, and provides dramatic views of the area. It can be reached from Leura, via the Mt Hay Road, which branches off the Great Western Highway. The road is pretty rough, although normal cars have been known to handle it if taken carefully. There may have been some deterioration in the condition of the road in recent times, however. In any case, walkers could walk to Mt Hay and camp at the picnic ground. It is a walk of around sixteen kilometres; once out of Leura, the road soon gets into the bush and it is not a bad walk.

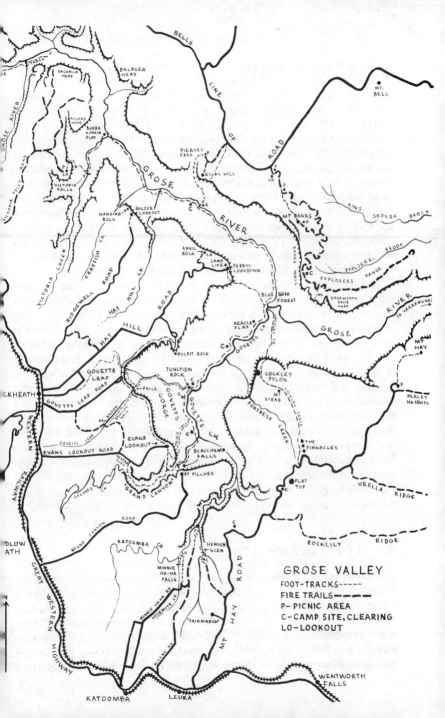

GROSE VALLEY

FOOT-TRACKS-----
FIRE TRAILS------
P-PICNIC AREA
C-CAMP SITE, CLEARING
LO-LOOKOUT

The first distinctive feature along the way is Flat Top, a flat-topped hill about nine kilometres up the road. A sign-posted jeep-track leads to the top of the hill, from which there are extensive views of the surrounding area and the Penrith plains, plus some glimpses of the walls of the Grose Valley.

Five minutes' walk past Flat Top, you come to the beginning of the Lockley Track, which will be dealt with later. There is a water-tank near the head of the track, and it has always been a reliable source of water in my experience. From the Lockley Track, it is six kilometres to the Mt Hay picnic ground — not an especially interesting walk. Immediately before the picnic site, you will see the fire trail down Hurley Heights. At the end of the trail there are views across the Kolonga Labyrinth, although whether the views are worth the long walk is debatable. Towards the end of this trail there is a turn-off on the south side which goes to a stream with a small pool, which can be handy if the water-tanks let you down.

Past the Hurley Heights trail, you come to the picnic ground, which is very basic. There is a stone fire-place but no excess of wood, a water-tank which in my experience has not been as reliable as the one at the Lockley Track, and enough room for one small tent and not much more. There is also a good view of Mt Hay and the Penrith Plains. At night the plains are covered in lights and you can make out the Centrepoint Tower in the distance. It would also be a great place to watch the sun come up.

From the picnic ground, a track leads to Mt Hay itself, about two kilometres away. There are some great views of the Grose as you approach the lower slopes of the mountain, but the views disappear as you get into the timber. The track was getting mildly overgrown the last time I was there, and there are some rocky stretches where a slight clamber is necessary, but it is not difficult to follow. At the top there is a CMA trig, but no views because of the trees. You would have to scrub-bash down to the edge of the cliffs to get views from the mountain itself; anyone not feeling that adventurous might do better to stick with the views on the lower slopes.

2. The Lockley Track

Branching off the Mt Hay Road, the Lockley Track provides some of the best views in the area. The first part of the track winds past the Pinnacles, three craggy rock formations on the east side of the track. It is possible to climb them in places. The track then proceeds through open heath, with some wooden sections, until it reaches Mt Stead. Between the Pinnacles and Mt Stead there are a couple of open spaces where camping would be possible, although there is, of course, no water. From Mt Stead, you come out of the final wooded section and get your first view of the Lockley Pylon, a pyramid-shaped hill perched right on the edge of the valley. The track goes past the Pylon, with a minor branch leading up to the top. It is worth going up to the top for the 360°view of the Grose and surrounding area — one of the best views you are ever likely to see.

From the Pylon, the track continues to the edge of the cliffs. There are some rocky sections where a little scrambling is necessary, but nothing too difficult. At the edge of the cliff, a silver arrow points to the pass where the track proceeds down into the valley. The track is harder to follow, in some places, then it used to be, because saplings have obscured it since the Great Fire of 1982 — unless some clearing work has been done more recently. However, follow the track carefully and within three-quarters of an hour or thereabouts you should be down at the Blue Gum Forest. The track is fairly steep, which makes for some fairly hard work with a backpack, but not too much trouble otherwise.

3. Neates Glen, the Grand Canyon

The Grand Canyon is a beautiful canyon where Greaves Creek flows from near Blackheath to Govetts Gorge. Although somewhat ineptly named in my opinion — it is nothing like its American namesake — it is a beautiful place rich in ferns, trees, moss-covered logs and the special atmosphere that only a rainforest area can create. A walk through the canyon can start at Neates Glen or Evans Lookout, but it is probably slightly easier to start at the former.

About three kilometres up the Evans Lookout Road, outside Blackheath, you will see the sign-posted Neates Glen picnic area where the track begins; the picnic area is equipped with taps, benches and fire-places. The track zigzags down the slopes for a while and eventually leads into Neates Glen, an attractive gully full of ferns and fern trees. The track is fairly steep but equipped with hand railings. Eventually you find yourself going down a flight of steps at the bottom of which you bear sharply to your right as you approach the canyon. The track levels off and becomes fairly undulating for a while, and includes a short tunnel cut through the rock. After you have worked your way along Greaves Creek a bit, through green and ferny surroundings, you come to the main part of the canyon, where only a philistine could refuse to linger for a while and take it all in.

When ready to proceed, continue through the canyon and after about five minutes you will come to a sign-posted parting of the ways. At this point, you can take the track (sign-posted) up to Evans Lookout or take the Rodriguez Pass into Govetts Gorge, but we will leave the latter for another section. The track up to Evans Lookout goes initially through some beautiful rainforest scenery that is well worth taking a long look at, complete with fern trees, stream, rock shelters and so on. Further on, it climbs the slopes and takes you into more of a dry eucalypt environment, providing an interesting contrast between the lush scenery of the gully and the drier woods up on the ridge. Eventually the track brings you to Evans Lookout, where you can enjoy a superb view of Govetts Gorge and the Grose Valley, looking north towards Mt Banks. The lookout is equipped with taps and shelters, although for some reason there was no running water the last time I was there. Further up the track, there is another picnic area with fire-places. Anyone who does not want to do the whole walk from Neates Glen (for which you should allow at least a few hours) could do an abbreviated version by going down from Evans Lookout and back up again: about fifteen minutes down and half an hour back up, for a fit walker. The track from the canyon up to Evans Lookout is fairly gradual as Grose Valley tracks go, and is one of the easier ways of getting out of the valley.

4.   Evans Lookout to Govetts Leap

The track from Evans Lookout to Govetts Leap provides an interesting and fairly undemanding walk of about three kilometres, with some good views along the way. The sign at the beginning of the track stipulates ninety minutes for the walk, but a fit walker could do it in fifty minutes without strain.

The track begins at the rough barbecue area just up the track from Evans Lookout, beside the signs saying *barbecues* and *toilets* (if they have not been vandalised by the time you read this). It immediately goes down a slope for some distance before levelling off; the track forks straightaway, but the two branches rejoin a bit further down, and are only a few metres apart in any case. In the long run the track undulates somewhat through the inevitable dry eucalypt scrub; you may see some signs of the burning from the Great Fire, but the bush has regenerated well. Eventually you go downhill to Govetts Leap Brook, at the spot where it flings itself over the cliff to create the waterfall named after Romaine Govett, the surveyor who discovered the falls. 'Leap' is a Welsh word for a sudden waterfall. Just before reaching the waterfall you will find a lookout with good views of the valley.

From Govetts Leap Brook it is uphill for a while before the track levels off to take you to Govetts Leap Lookout. Here you will find a superb view, looking east along the length of the Grose Valley; in my opinion this is a truly first-class view by any standards and is probably the finest view in the Blue Mountains. It certainly leaves the Three Sisters for dead. There

THE FALL OF WATER
WAS NAMED
GOVETT'S LEAP
FROM THE CIRCUMSTANCE OF
WILLIAM ROMAINE. GOVETT.
ASSISTANT SURVEYOR.
"FIRST HAVING COME UPON THE SPOT"
IN JUNE, 1831.
BLACKHEATH RESERVES TRUST.
1935.

The memorial to Govett, who discovered the falls that are now named after him

are numerous features that can be picked out, like Mt Hay, the Lockley Pylon, Pulpit Rock, the Explorers Range and Govetts Leap itself. Spend a bit of time on this view — it is worth every minute. Nearby, you will see the picnic ground, where there are taps, shelters, fire-places and so forth. From here, Govetts Leap Road leads back to Blackheath.

5. Govetts Leap to Pulpit Rock

At Govetts Leap Lookout you will see the signs pointing to Pulpit Rock and other places — the last time I was there, they had arrows pointing in opposite directions, so be sure to go to the left and not the right. The track proceeds gradually downhill to Popes Glen Creek, at which point you cross to the east side of the creek and go uphill. After this, the track follows the cliff fairly closely for a couple of kilometres, providing views of Govetts Gorge and part of the east arm of the Grose. Eventually you will see Pulpit Rock up ahead, a distinctive rock formation about halfway down the cliff. The track eventually joins another track to the lookout above Pulpit Rock; go down to the lookout for some good views of the valley. From the main lookout, another track leads to a secondary lookout further down.

Going back in the other direction, that is, north, the track leads up to a shelter with some rudimentary picnic facilities and a water-tank which had a broken tap the last time I was there, but presumably this will not be the case forever. Past the shelter, the track joins a turning-circle from where you can go up to Hat Hill Road, which leads to Perrys Lookdown or back to Blackheath.

6. Perrys Lookdown and Anvil Rock

The Hat Hill Road provides access to two notable lookouts, Perrys

Lookdown and Anvil Rock. The latter is reached first via a turn-off to the left, or north, about a kilometre before Perrys Lookdown. As you go along the turn-off towards Anvil Rock, you will see the rock silhouetted against the sky, and will be able to see how appropriately named it is. At the end of the road there is a picnic ground with a water-tank and fire-place. A track leads up to the top of the rock, from which you have some superb views of the Grose. The view to the west is particularly good, with the features on the north wall of the valley being very easy to identify. Mt Banks, Rigby Hill and the Grose River can be seen easily, as well as the tracks between Rigby Hill and the Bell Road, which can also be made out in places. To the east you have a clear view of Mt Hay.

Back at the picnic ground, another sign-posted track leads to the 'wind-eroded cave', which is just a large rock shelter reached after about five minutes' walk. The area is sometimes used by abseilers.

After Anvil Rock, proceed to Perrys Lookdown, where there is a large camp ground on the north side of the road. One simple way to enjoy the Grose would be to spend a couple of nights at this camp ground and do day-walks around the cliff tracks. The lookout is just past the camp ground, slightly down a track. The feature most immediately apparent is the Banks Wall, which is the cliff formation below Mt Banks, but you can also make out Mt Hay and the Lockley Pylon, and can even see the Lockley Track winding up Du Faurs Buttress. Banks Wall looks particularly good at the end of the day when it catches the warm light of the afternoon sun, but for my money Anvil Rock is the better of the two lookouts.

7. The Braeside Walk

The Braeside Walk branches off the cliff track between Evans Lookout and Govetts Leap Lookout, and goes to the outskirts of Blackheath. The track begins where the cliff track comes to Govetts Leap Brook. On the east side of the Brook you will see the track going upstream; there used to be a sign saying 'Braeside Walk' but there is now a new one saying 'Braeside Picnic Area'. The track follows the Brook pretty closely, passing some small cascades and going through some very dry, open and partly grassy scrubland, with some nice grey gums. Only about seven minutes' walk along, you pass a rather rundown picnic spot by the side of the Brook.

Further upstream, the scrub gets denser along the Brook and after another five or ten minutes you go up the slope a bit to arrive at another small picnic area, with benches and a table — this time in rather better condition. Nearby, there is a bit of a pool where a weir has been built across the Brook; just upstream of the pool, you cross on a footbridge and find another set of benches and a table on the other side (you're never short of a seat on this walk). From here, some steps lead up the slope to a service road, where there are numerous signs announcing the presence of the Braeside Walk, so you will have no trouble finding it if you start the walk at this end. Turning right, you follow the service road uphill through dry eucalypt woods for about ten minutes, before arriving at Braeside Street, where there are more signs. From here it is about twenty minutes' walk into Blackheath. The Braeside Walk is not an especially spectacular walk in its own right, but is an alternative way of getting to the cliff track without having to walk through the streets all the way.

8.   Govetts Leap to Junction Rock

From Govetts Leap Lookout, a track zigzags down the cliff to provide one of the more dramatic ways of entering the Grose Valley. From the signs mentioned in Section 5, go to the right and follow the track as it works its way along and down the cliff. The track is narrow and rocky but with plenty of railings and steel steps where necessary, so no-one is going to have any trouble. A steep walk like this, of course, is not for the aged or infirm.

As you go along, you get some good views of Govetts Leap itself, providing some good vantage points from which to photograph the waterfall, for any budding photographers. Eventually the track takes you to the base of the falls, after a walk of forty-five minutes or so. From here, it is a fairly solid and undulating walk of about one hour to get to Junction Rock. The track goes through some quite rich forest with cascades where the track crosses Govetts Leap Brook, making for quite an interesting walk, going roughly parallel to the Brook. Before reaching Junction Rock, you cross the Brook at a broad, rocky section where there are one or two arrows painted on the rocks, and complete the walk on the north side of the Brook to reach Junction Rock. The latter is a flat rock near the junction of the Brook and Govetts Creek. Anyone starting the walk at this end should remember that the track is found on the *north* side of the Brook, since the sign-post nearby makes it look as though the track can be picked up on the south side.

Intending walkers should also remember that the track up to Govetts Leap is *extremely* step and not the easiest way to get out of the valley.

9.   Evans Lookout Bridle Trail

Following the track from Evans Lookout to the Grand Canyon, not far down there is a bridle trail that branches off on the east side and goes down to the valley floor. It emerges at a point only about fifteen minutes' walk south of Junction Rock, and is shown as a foot-track on the Mt Wilson topographic map. For some strange reason, the NPWS has had this trail closed to walkers for some time, perhaps to leave room for the horses, who commonly freak out at the slightest sign of us big, vicious bushwalkers. At the bottom of the track, where it joins the Rodriguez Pass, there is or was a sign saying that the track could be used by horseriders as a way out of the valley when Govetts Creek was in flood — which couldn't be all that often. The only other sign is a low, wooden post in the ground, at the foot of the track, with an arrow pointing along the Rodriguez Pass, giving us all a gentle hint to by-pass the bridle trail. Nevertheless, it happens that this trail is relatively gradual in its grade, as Grose Valley tracks go, and is one of the easier ways out of the valley. It is worth keeping it in mind, for people who find they have overestimated themselves and want a relatively easy way out. It is certainly easier than the tracks to Govetts Leap and Perrys Lookdown.

10. Perrys Lookdown to Blue Gum Forest

From Perrys Lookdown, a track continues down into the valley, arriving at the famous Blue Gum Forest. This is one of the steeper tracks in the valley and can be quite hard work even when going downhill, especially if you have a backpack. I have not had the dubious honour of going uphill along this track, since I have always made a point of avoiding it; it is not recommended, especially for backpackers.

The track starts off innocently enough with an average sort of downhill grade, then flattens out for a while as it winds a bit further around the slope. After that, it starts to plunge downhill in no uncertain manner, and it can be a steep walk of about an hour before you finally get to the Blue Gum Forest. The track has been upgraded since the fire of '82 and the bottom part is now clearer, and more clearly sign-posted, than before. Once at the bottom, you can enjoy the charms of the beautiful Blue Gum Forest and the Grose River — a good place to cool off if you go there in summer. Camping is now prohibited in the Blue Gum because people were trampling the saplings, leading to the possibility that the whole forest would one day die out. It is possible, on occasion, to see horses and cattle grazing in the forest. Some of the horses had been left behind from coal-mining operations in the valley, while others are allowed to graze there by landowners in the Blackheath area. These days they are being shot by the NPWS because of the damage they do to the foliage. They are most likely to be seen early in the morning.

Some masochists like to do a day-walk from Perrys Lookdown to the Blue Gum Forest and back up again; in this case, I suggest allowing at least one hour for the walk down and at least twice as much for the return walk.

From the Blue Gum Forest it is, of course, possible to do a long walk downstream along the Grose River, eventually coming out at the spot known as Yarramundi, just a few kilometres from the Nepean River. I must confess that I have not done this walk myself, but I gather that the old track is now somewhat overgrown and the walking can be slow and rough. Nevertheless, this walk might be worth considering for those hardy types who really want to get away from civilisation for a few days or more and have the world to themselves. From the Blue Gum Forest to Yarramundi would be forty-odd kilometres of virtually pure wilderness that would probably take at least four days to cover, given how slow the progress can be in such conditions. About three-quarters of the way down there is a walking track up to the fire trail on Faulconbridge Ridge, presenting an alternative way of leaving or entering the river area. Fit walkers could also co⎯⎯⎯⎯⎯⎯⎯⎯ k from Faulconbridge to the river and then on to Richmond ⎯⎯⎯⎯⎯ thirty kilometres or so. Many experienced walkers tend ⎯⎯⎯⎯⎯ ion on the Colo River, the supposed wilderness paradis⎯ ⎯⎯⎯⎯⎯; but I would think that the east end of the Grose, virtually ⎯⎯⎯⎯, would probably present a wilderness experience compa⎯⎯⎯⎯⎯ ne Colo, and without the access problems associated with th⎯⎯⎯⎯⎯ Colo area.

Really ambitious types could also consider the ⎯⎯⎯⎯⎯ k: walking the whole length of the Grose River, from the old ⎯⎯⎯⎯ g Engineers Track near Bell to the Nepean River at the other enu. ⎯⎯⎯ ould be a walk of about sixty kilometres, about three-quarters of which would be virtually trackless. It would be strictly for fit walkers who do not mind roughing it, and would probably take the best part of a week. It would certainly be a good way to get away from it all, for those who are fit enough for it.

11. The Rodriguez Pass

At the bottom of the track from Evans Lookout to the Grand Canyon, the Rodriguez Pass begins its journey into Govetts Gorge. The track is sign-posted, with signs saying 'Rodriguez Pass' and 'Beauchamp Falls'. The latter is a waterfall formed by Greaves Creek, only about ten minutes' walk further east of the Grand Canyon. To begin the walk, cross Greaves Creek on the rocks and pick the track up immediately on the south side of the creek. About five minutes' walk down, you cross the creek again at a rather nice rainforested spot, then continue further downhill through some rocky stretches to arrive at Beauchamp Falls. There is a reasonable view of the gorge along the way, just before you plunge down the slope to the falls.

Beauchamp Falls can be seen from the track but you might like to clamber on the rocks to get a closer view — they are worth looking at, and worth photographing. From the falls, the track continues downhill for another quarter of an hour or so before crossing Greaves Creek again at a wide, flat rocky section. There are some cascades here that make a good picture, if any photographers are interested. For the next kilometre, the track follows the creek through some rich forest, similar to rainforest if not quite true rainforest, before crossing yet again to the other side. At this stage you are near the junction of Greaves Creek and Govetts Creek, and the track now follows the latter for the rest of the walk to Blue Gum Forest. Around here, just north of the junction of the two creeks, there is a rough camp-site that could come in handy for some people. It is not one of the authorised camp-sites in the valley, but they are not always there just when you want them.

The track now undulates along the west side of Govetts Creek for another one and a half kilometres on the way to Junction Rock. You should see the entrance to the bridle trail described in Section 9, and after another fifteen minutes or so you are at the junction of Govetts Creek and Govetts Leap Brook, and Junction Rock — altogether, about one and a half to two hours' walk from Beauchamp Falls. After crossing the Brook on some rocks, you go up the slope and find another camp-site that could be handy on occasion. From here, it is about an hour's walk to Acacia Flat, the large, authorised camp ground just south of the Blue Gum Forest. Along the way, you will pass through Fortress Creek Flat, another authorised camp ground, which was in something of a mess after the Great Fire but is recovering well. Acacia Flat is very spacious and is only about ten minutes' walk from the Blue Gum Forest, which makes it a good place to camp for anyone who wants to enjoy the charms of the area.

12. Blue Gum Forest to Victoria Falls Lookout

This is a stretch of some eight kilometres, featuring a track that has always been a little rough. However, reconstruction has been going on since the Great Fire, and the track will probably improve if it has not already done so. From Blue Gum, the track proceeds north, staying on the west side of the Grose River. The Mt Wilson topographic map for some reason has always shown the track crossing to the east side for a while, just north of the Blue Gum Forest, but it can be followed all the way on the west side.

The first four kilometres are pretty straightforward, with no particular distinguishing features or confusing factors. Progress may be relatively slow unless the track has been upgraded, but basically you just follow the river, going upstream in a generally north-west direction.

At the four-kilometre mark you come to the Hungerford Track, which leads to Pierces Pass and the Bell Range, but we can leave that for another section. This turn-off has been newly sign-posted as part of the track reconstruction, so you should have no trouble seeing it. The scenery through this area is a mixture of river scenes, rich forest and views of the steep walls of the valley.

Slightly to the west of the Hungerford Track, you go past a rough camp-site that could be useful for anyone doing a camping trip in the area. About a kilometre further west, you come to a spot that can be a little disorienting for those who do not already know the track: this is the spot where the track reaches Hat Hill Creek. The Mt Wilson map shows the track crossing the creek in a straight line, from east to west, but it actually makes a sharp turn to the right as it goes down the slope towards the creek; you then cross on the rocks, follow the track uphill a bit and do another turn before the track straightens out to proceed west, after which you can see the Grose River clearly over to your right. Lest you think I am being too picky in making this point, let me explain that I personally found this spot a bit confusing when I first went through, because initially it looks as though you are crossing the Grose River — which, of course, you do not do at this stage.

About half a kilometre further west, the track fords Crayfish Creek, from where, if you look carefully at the cliffs to the south-west, you can see the Hanging Rock, which will be dealt with in detail in a later section. After this, another two kilometres' walk will bring you to Burra Korain Flat, a grassy area to the west side of the junction of the Grose River and Victoria Creek, although it is not marked on the topographic map. The new edition of the map, incidentally, shows the track always staying on the south side of the junction, but you actually cross on the rocks to get to Burra Korain Flat. From there, if you are not camping, you can pick up the track again on the west side of the Flat and then cross to the south side of Victoria Creek.

From here, the track has already been upgraded and the way is quite clear. The track provides a pleasant walk upstream along Victoria Creek, going past cascades and through rainforest sections. After about two kilometres you come to Victoria Falls. You must leave the main track and walk on the rocks to get a good look at the falls, which tumble over a spectacular rock shelf and are worth having a good look at. If you go there in summer, you may appreciate the opportunity to swim in the pool at the base of the falls.

From the falls, the track winds fairly steeply up the slopes to reach Victoria Falls Lookout. Not far up, there is a sign-posted turn-off that provides a glimpse of some cascades along the creek. After that, the walk gets fairly steep and would be difficult for the unfit, especially once you go through the pass in the cliffs. At the top, the walk is rewarded by a good view from Victoria Falls Lookout, taking in mostly the Bell Range with features like Dalpura Head and Asgard Head. The view is probably at its best when the sun is coming up.

Just above the lookout, the track leads to a picnic area with a water-tank, and from there it is about five kilometres to Mt Victoria. Fit walkers could consider a long day-walk from Perrys Lookdown to Victoria Falls Lookout, via the Grose River, which would require, I think, *at least* six hours of walking time, not counting the time spent getting to Perrys Lookdown and from Victoria Falls Lookout to Mt Victoria. It would be an advantage to get a lift to Perrys Lookdown.

The view of the Grose Valley from Victoria Falls Lookout

13.   Pierces Pass

From the Grose River track, you cross on the rocks where the turn-off for Pierces Pass is sign-posted. The track goes up the slope to a camp-site, and then continues further up. It climbs fairly steeply in a roughly north-west direction, providing good views of the valley walls as it ascends the slope. Near the top, the track goes into Pierces Ravine and draws alongside Pierces Creek, where it comes to a beautiful spot called Fairy Grotto. This is a shady rainforest spot along Pierces Creek, sign-posted and easily reached by a turn-off from the main track. It is worth stopping to look at the Grotto, and it would make a good place for a rest if walking uphill.

From around Fairy Grotto, the track goes uphill and out of the ravine until it reaches an old picnic area with a water-tank. This spot was falling apart when I last saw it but it may be upgraded with the work going on in the valley at the time of writing. From this spot, a service road goes about a kilometre to the Bell Road, where there is another water-tank. Pierces Pass is sign-posted at the Bell Road, although the sign-post is not as conspicuous as the one for our next stop, Mt Banks.

14.   Mt Banks

Mt Banks is one of the dominant features of the Bell Range and the Grose Valley, which it overlooks. It can be reached via an unsealed road which turns off the Bell Road, and which is quite conspicuously sign-posted. Not far down the road, you pass a small picnic area with a water-tank, and opposite is a turn-off that leads, after only a few metres, to a spot from which there is a reasonable view of Mt Banks and part of the valley. About three quarters of a kilometre further down the road, you come to the main picnic area, which is situated to the north-west side of the mountain; it is quite large, and is equipped with water-tank, tables and benches.

Near the picnic ground, the road is closed by a locked gate; not far from the gate is a monument to the explorer Caley, who made one of the early attempts to cross the Blue Mountains, and behind the monument is the track to the top of Mt Banks. The track goes up the slope through very dry, heath-like undergrowth, providing views of the Bell Range and Mt Tomah in particular. About three quarters of the way up, the track goes into the timbered area on top of the mountain, and the scenery changes quite dramatically. From open heath it changes abruptly to shady forest and grassy slopes, as the top of the mountain is a basalt plug that creates a vastly different soil from that on the lower slopes. The track proceeds to the King George trig on top, but unfortunately there are no views because of the

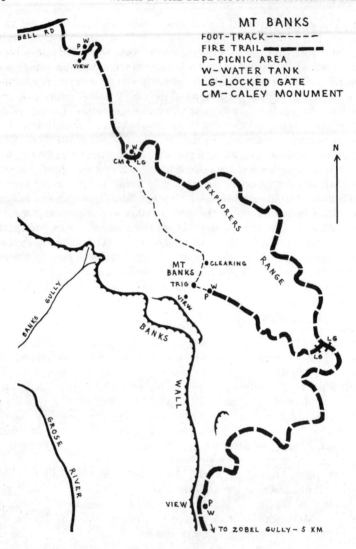

MT BANKS
FOOT-TRACK ------
FIRE TRAIL ▬ ▬ ▬ ▬
P - PICNIC AREA
W - WATER TANK
LG - LOCKED GATE
CM - CALEY MONUMENT

N

BELL RD

P W
VIEW

P W
CM LG

EXPLORERS

RANGE

CLEARING

MT
BANKS
TRIG
VIEW
P W

LG

LG

BANKS GULLY

BANKS

WALL

GROSE

RIVER

VIEW P
W

↓ TO ZOBEL GULLY - 5 KM

timber. If you go down the slopes somewhat below the trig, you will come to a clear spot from which there are views of the valley, looking towards Govetts Gorge. The views are still a little hemmed in by the trees, but are quite reasonable.

On your way to the trig, you will notice a picnic area to the east of the main track. This is equipped with a water-tank, and from the picnic area you can follow a service road that goes down the east slope of the mountain to join the road from the picnic area mentioned above. This main road continues for another five or six kilometres along the Explorers Range and is worth having a look at. Along the south-east slopes of the mountain, the road passes through some interesting scenery with craggy gums towering above the road, and some glimpses of Mt Hay in the distance. Directly south of Mt Banks, the road goes close to the edge of Banks Wall, and at this point there is a basic picnic area with a tank. From the cliff there is an excellent view of the valley, looking west towards Asgard Head — a good view at the end of the day. This would be a good place to spend a night, although it might be a little exposed.

From the picnic area, the road continues for another three or four kilometres. On the west side of David Crevasse there is a turn-off that goes to the cliff, passing a rough clearing that could be used for camping, although there is no water. A few kilometres further on, the road comes to an end just short of Mt Caley. This road provides some good views which I think make it more rewarding than the walk up Mt Banks, although the latter provides the interesting contrast between the heath of the lower slopes and the forest on top.

15.   Balzer Lookout and the Hanging Rock

The Balzer Lookout sits on the south edge of the Grose Valley, more or less north-east of Blackheath. It can be reached via Ridgewell Road, just north of Blackheath Station, and offers excellent views of the Grose, as well as being close to the Hanging Rock, a rock formation that juts out from the valley walls.

From the beginning of Ridgewell Road, it is about six and a half kilometres to the lookout, passing through dry eucalypt woods along Burramoko Ridge. Anyone who does not have transport would find that it is a reasonable, though not exciting, walk, and it is possible to camp at the lookout, although you must take your own water. The road comes to an end just short of the lookout, and a track leads up the slope. The ground levels off among eucalypts as the track approaches the edge of the cliff, where there are good views to the east, north and north-west. Mt Banks is featured to the east, and, further in the distance, it is possible to gain a glimpse of the Penrith plains and even the City of Sydney. If you are there at the end of the day, you can see all the lights from the plains to the city — probably one of the best lookouts around the Grose.

To find the Hanging Rock, walk straight ahead from the lookout, bearing

slightly to the left as you follow the slopes down along the edge of the cliff.
A rough track leads down among the heath and if you keep going straight
ahead you will come to a spot where you are looking directly down at the
Hanging Rock. None of this is sign-posted — not even the lookout — but
if you wak ahead as described you should find the rock, which is a wedge-
shaped formation hanging out from the cliff. Some people have described
it as 'incredible', but this writer is not so easy to impress; personally, I
think the lookout is better than the rock. From where you first see the rock,
it is possible to work your way down and get a closer look if you wish to.

Balzer Lookout may not be an authorised camp-site as such, but there
is nothing to stop anyone from spending a night there, since there is some
open space around the trees near the lookout. There is some firewood
around, and you may see the remains of a camp-fire. This lookout is a good
place to watch the sun come up, as well as the lights in the distance at night.
A full moon tops it off nicely.

16.   Henson Glen, Minnie Ha-Ha Falls

The north side of Katoomba is a maze of creeks and gullies, some of which
have been dammed to provide water for the residential areas, and all of
which end up in the Grose Valley one way or another. Two of the main
watercourses of Govetts Gorge — Greaves Creek and Govetts Creek —
start in this area between Blackheath and Leura, and, in spite of their
proximity to the built-up areas, there are several spots that are relatively
untouched and which offer opportunities for exploration and sightseeing.
There are, not surprisingly, some power-lines to be encountered along the
way in some places, but these are a minor detail and in no way detract from
the enjoyment of the walks. Two of the most distinctive features are Henson
Glen and Minnie Ha-Ha Falls, which can be linked up into one walk which
could be done in one day by a reasonably fit walker, or treated as two
separate walks.

Starting from Leura Station, walk east down the Great Western Highway
and turn up the Mt Hay Road, which is only about half a kilometre from
the station. Following the Mt Hay Road for about three kilometres, you
will come to a fire trail on the west side of the road, five minutes' walk
past the 'Fairmarch' property. There is an old sign at the beginning of the
fire trail; the original lettering has long faded, but 'Henson Glen' has been
printed on the sides of the post. The fire trail winds through the scrub for
just over a kilometre, following a spur that juts from the Mt Hay Range
and goes parallel to Govetts Creek on its way to Govetts Gorge. Along the
way, you go under some power-lines supported by wooden poles, until the

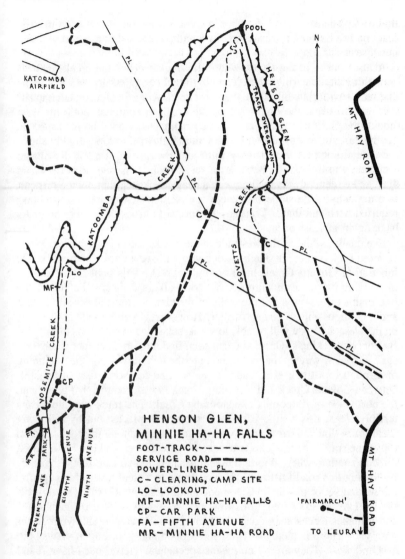

HENSON GLEN,
MINNIE HA-HA FALLS
FOOT-TRACK ------
SERVICE ROAD ===
POWER-LINES _PL___
C - CLEARING, CAMP SITE
LO - LOOKOUT
MF - MINNIE HA-HA FALLS
CP - CAR PARK
FA - FIFTH AVENUE
MR - MINNIE HA-HA ROAD

road starts to fizzle out a little further along near another set of power-lines, this time on steel towers. Where the road starts to taper off, you will see a track that continues down the slope and curls around the north side of the spur to join Govetts Creek. The track is not shown on the Katoomba topographic map, but this map is worth having in any case for anyone doing this walk. The track is a little faint in some places, but if you keep in mind that you are heading towards the creek and basically downstream you will not lose it for long.

At the bottom of the slope, where the track reaches the creek, there is something of a clearing where camping would be possible, and this is the last such spot for a while since there are no clearings in Henson Glen itself. Around this area, the track crosses the creek to continue along the west side of the glen, which will already be getting steep-sided by the time you get this far. As you go further on, the track follows the slope slightly above the creek, but gets increasingly faint and overgrown until it disappears completely and the walk becomes a scrub-bash. It is one of those walks that can be relatively demanding with a heavy backpack, but not too difficult as a day-walk. The slopes are rocky and scrubby, with some scrambling required here and there. You may be forced to cross the creek and cross back again at least once.

Eventually, while on the west side of the creek, you come to a long, moss-covered rock on the far side of which you will see a pool which marks the junction of Govetts Creek and Katoomba Creek. This pool might make a nice swimming hole in summer, but for walkers it means the end of the line in this direction, since the walls of the glen are quite sheer at this spot and it is impossible to go any further. However, if you look up above you, on the west side, you will be able to see a rock ledge that ascends the slopes. By double-tracking slightly, you can soon find a reasonable spot where you can work your way up the rocks and onto the ledge, which is the beginning of a rough foot-track. The track curves around the north face of the spur between Govetts Creek and Yosemite Creek, a watercourse that goes from the north side of Katoomba to Katoomba Creek. The track is by no means terribly clear; it is a little vague and scrappy in places, but by following it carefully you can eventually work your way up among the rocks and on top of the spur. The track is clear once you are on top, and can be followed directly south to where it joins a maintenance road that runs along the spur. Following this road further south, you come to a steel tower that supports the second set of power-lines you encountered along the first fire trail off the Mt Hay Road. Around this tower there is a great deal of open space and it makes a reasonable place to camp, so long as you take your water with you. There is plenty of firewood around and good, open views both east and west. They are by no means spectacular views, but I have found it is pleasant to camp in places with an open ambience. As far as the walk so far is concerned, I would not say that it is for experienced walkers only, but obviously it is messy enough in some places to be disqualified as an average Sunday stroll.

Continuing further south along the spur, you will want the Katoomba

The pool at the north end of Henson Glen

map to help you find your way through the jumble of roads and turn-offs that lies ahead. Passing a couple of turn-offs that you will see on the map, you come to a fork where you must take the right-hand or west road that goes down the slope towards Yosemite Creek. This is all shown on the Katoomba map, although I found that the western turn-off is actually more like a continuation of the main road rather than the sharp turn drawn on the map. Nevertheless, following this road down the slope, you turn north at the bottom and, a bit further along, come to a large turning circle and car-park where people park before going on to Minnie Ha-Ha Falls. A sign at the far end of the car-park indicates the track to the falls. The track follows Yosemite Creek, passing some cascades, then bears north-east around the falls to arrive at a lookout that provides a good view of the waterfall. At the far, or north, end of the lookout, there is another track that winds down to the base of the falls. It is only a five-minute walk down to the base and it is worth going down to have a better look. The base of the falls is a good place to take pictures, although a wide-angle lens is needed to fit the waterfall in at such close quarters.

From here, there is no other track leading out of the area, so you must retrace your steps. Once you get back to the original road you came down, you have the choice of heading down Minnie Ha-Ha Road towards Katoomba; or, if you prefer a bit more bushwalking, you can use the map to follow the fire trails to Eighth Avenue and Clydebank Road, on the north side of Leura, and then on to Leura Station. I found that the jumble of dirt roads around Eighth and Ninth Avenues is not quite as clear as it looks on the map, but it makes life more interesting.

Minnie Ha-Ha Falls

5. Mt Wilson to Deep Pass

North of the Bell Range, the terrain gets increasingly rugged and is criss-crossed by creeks and rivers with sheer sandstone walls, forming a veritable honeycomb of canyons. The exception is, of course, Mt Wilson, the island in the wilderness, where visitors can enjoy sights that range from rhododendrons to rainforest. A number of tracks create simple walks that take in caves, creeks, waterfalls, lookouts and rainforest and which are suitable for virtually all walkers.

Immediately north of Mt Wilson, the ridges slope down to the Wallangambe River — the end of civilisation and the beginning of the wilderness in the truest sense. Few tracks penetrate this world, which looks deceptively mild and undulating when seen at a distance from Mt Wilson. Fire trails touch the edges around Bell and the Clarence Colliery, but to go much further requires considerable bushwalking experience and skill at navigation.

On the east side of Lithgow, more fire trails provide access to the intriguing world of Deep Pass, on the northern boundary of the national park. At Deep Pass, between Bungleboori Creek and Nayook Creek, a spacious camp ground lies adjacent to an Aboriginal site, with a walking track through the pass and another track into the jungle-like world of Nayook Creek. Those prepared to do some clambering can also find their way up Mt Norris and, from there, expert navigators could consider extended treks along Railmotor Ridge and into the wilderness of the Wollemi National Park. More than most other parts of the Blue Mountains National Park, the northern section provides the opportunity to enjoy the feeling of having the world to yourself, if you have enough experience to be able to handle it.

1. Mt Wilson

Mt Wilson has been described by some as our little piece of England, and certainly has a character of its own that is not much like the usual Australian landscape. The proliferation of gardens, pines and fern trees gives it a degree of greenery that is attractive and distinctive in an Australian context. To walk around Mt Wilson is to feel that you are in a place that is quite a little world of its own, and a place where only the privileged get to live.

There are several spots in Mt Wilson that are worth looking at and which can make for some pleasant walking. There are also a few picnic grounds that provide reasonable facilities and which can double as camping grounds

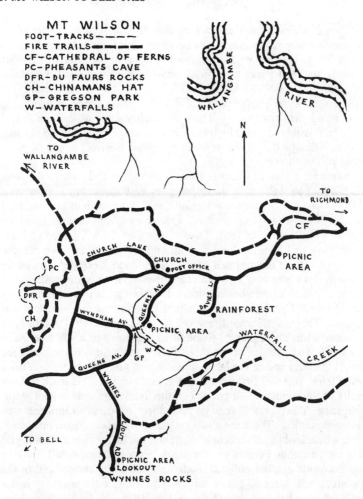

MT WILSON
FOOT-TRACKS — — — —
FIRE TRAILS ■■■ ■■■ ■■■
CF — CATHEDRAL OF FERNS
PC — PHEASANTS CAVE
DFR — DU FAURS ROCKS
CH — CHINAMANS HAT
GP — GREGSON PARK
W — WATERFALLS

for anyone who wants to spend a few days in the area. Anyone who likes
long walks could consider a walk from the Bell Road at the east end of
the Mt Wilson road, going right through the Mt Wilson area via Bowens
Creek and on towards Bell. I have not personally done this walk, and have
found that walks along roads are not always the most fascinating, but it
would be easy and undemanding, and would offer a lot of good mountain
scenery along the way, since the elevated position of Mt Wilson provides
many glimpses of the surrounding ranges. There are enough picnic grounds,
starting at Bowens Creek, to provide places to camp.

For shorter walks, however, we could start arbitrarily at the western end, where the first stop is Wynnes Rocks Lookout. This is at the end of Wynnes Lookout Road, off Queens Avenue, and is right on the edge of the Blue Mountains National Park; it provides views of the ranges and mountains to the south, particularly Mt Banks and Mt Hay. The view is fairly expansive but, to be blunt, is not all that spectacular, although it could be an interesting place to watch the sun come up. There is a shelter and a water-tank so that it would be possible to spend a night there if you especially wanted to catch the dawn, although the picnic areas further down the road would be more pleasant places to stay.

To continue, return to Queens Avenue, head east and, where the road bends north, you will see a track that goes east and down a slope to a footbridge across a tributary to Waterfall Creek. The patch of scrub around this bridge is known as Gregson Park, a rather extravagant name given the limited size of the piece of land. Anyone going by car will have to bypass Gregson Park and take the long way around via Wyndham Avenue, the Mt Wilson road and the east half of Queens Avenue, the latter road being ingeniously split into two separate roads that have the same name.

On the east side of the abovementioned footbridge, a dirt road leads up to the Waterfall Creek picnic area, where there are several shelters and fire-places. There is adequate firewood, by and large, even if you have to look around a bit. These picnic grounds are maintained on a volunteer basis by the locals and one can only ask visitors to assist in keeping the place clean. At the west end of the picnic area, where you first come to it from Gregson Park, you will find a track that goes downhill. This track follows the gully of the tributary you crossed on the footbridge, and is well worth investigating. You do not have to go far before you are in a rainforest area that is quite magical. There are also a couple of waterfalls, small and large, that are worth looking at; a couple of minor tracks provide access if you have a look around. Further on, the track bears east and uphill, making a loop alongside another gully to finally emerge at the eastern end of the picnic area, near a set of public toilets. The track, unfortunately, is not sign-posted at either end, but at the east end you will find it behind the eastern-most of *two* sets of toilets that you will see.

Where you re-emerge at the picnic area, you are back in Queens Avenue (the eastern half of it). Further explorations proceed by heading up Queens Avenue and turning east at the main road which has a public park on its east side. Further along, the next stop is Davies Lane, on the south side of the main road. A few hundred metres down Davies Lane, there are some beautiful stretches of rainforest on both sides. The section on the west side of the road is, unfortunately, private property and is fenced off with barbed wire. On the east side, however, where the fences come to an end, there

The rather quaint St George's Church, Mt Wilson

Vines entwined around tree trunks, the Cathedral of Ferns

is a stretch of forest that is open to all and you can wander around to your heart's content. This particular piece of forest leads downhill to Waterfall Creek, thus providing considerable scope for walking around. I did not try to go all the way down to the creek, but presumably the undergrowth would get richer, and possibly thicker, as you went further down. Since there are no developed tracks, beginners should make a point of keeping their bearings, although if they get lost they would simply have to turn around and go back uphill again. Good walking shoes would be worthwhile.

About a kilometre east of Davies Lane, along the main road, lies one of the best known features of Mt Wilson — the Cathedral of Ferns. This unique patch of forest occupies a long, oval area on the slopes of a hill, and is a real wonderland of fern trees and hanging vines. There are several tracks through the area, with sign-posted entrances leading from the main road, and it is certainly worth spending an hour or so wandering around. Photographers will find plenty to take pictures of. I should add that there is a very spacious picnic area immediately before the Cathedral of Ferns, on the east side of the road, with water-tanks, shelters, fire-places and firewood.

Doubletracking westwards along the main road, if you bypass Queens Avenue you soon come to the centre of Mt Wilson (such as it is), where the post office and church are situated. At the post office you will see a large noticeboard and painted map of the Mt Wilson area, showing the various features and walking tracks. St George's Church of England, just past the post office, is worth a look, being a rather quaint and even eccentric construction of fibro, surrounded by fern trees. It makes a pretty picture.

At the side of the church is Church Lane, which could be bypassed unless you are determined to see every nook and cranny. About three-quarters of a kilometre further down the main road is a war memorial and the local school; in between them is a fire trail which leads to a well-known track that leads in turn to the Wallangambe River. Some people use this as a starting point for li-loing down the Wallangambe to the Colo River. I have not done this myself, but have been told that the going is excruciatingly slow, due to the amount of scrub blocking the Wallangambe. My informant told me he made almost no progress in three days.

Just past the school is the Bushfire Brigade Station, and at this point there is a sign-posted turn-off to the Du Faurs Rocks Lookout, which frankly is not worth seeing but which happens to be on the way to Pheasants Cave. The lookout at least has some Aboriginal axe-grinding grooves, and could be a good place to watch the sun go down, since it faces west. On the way to the lookout you pass a couple of fire trails on both north and south sides of the road, and just before reaching the lookout area you will see a foot-track on the north side of the road. Follow this track downhill and it goes around in a zigzagging kind of way, eventually coming out opposite the rock shelter known as Pheasants Cave. There are some hand railings along the way to make it easier and no-one should have any trouble negotiating the track, although it gets a little soggy towards the cave. The cave itself is not all that dramatic, but it is surrounded by rainforest and this is what makes the walk worth doing.

When you first descend the track from near Du Faurs Lookout, you will see a turn-off on your left that leads to a rock formation laughingly known as Chinamans Hat. The track is, however, a bit vague in places, with much doubling back on itself, and if you can actually find something that looks like a Chinamans Hat, or anyone else's hat, you will be doing very well. Altogether, not a highly recommended walk, except for those who like investigating vague tracks.

After the tour of Du Faurs Lookout, one thing remains: on the way to the lookout you pass a fire trail on the north side of the road. This curves around the northern outskirts of Mt Wilson for a few kilometres and emerges at the west end of the Cathedral of Ferns. If it fits your itinerary to go back that way, this fire trail is a very pleasant walk passing through some attractive forest, and with its share of fern trees; it makes an agreeable way to go back to the Cathedral of Ferns if you wish to. I should add, of course, that Mt Wilson is famous for its gardens, which are open to the public, normally

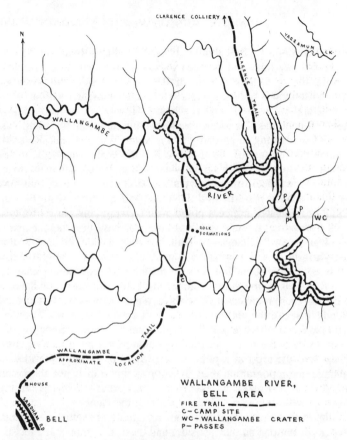

WALLANGAMBE RIVER,
BELL AREA
FIRE TRAIL ━━━━
C - CAMP SITE
WC - WALLANGAMBE CRATER
P - PASSES

for a small fee. I have not attempted to cover them here because they do not fit the theme of bushland and because I personally have no love at all for gardens, but many people would find them worth a visit.

2. Wallangambe River

The Wallangambe and its surrounding area, known as the Wallangambe Wilderness, make up a part of the Blue Mountains National Park that is undeveloped and untouched; probably the largest wilderness area in the entire park. This, of course, is a double-edged sword, meaning that there are no tracks and you have to be a good navigator if you want to go far into the area. The western end, however, is accessible via fire trails from Bell and the Clarence Colliery road, and this is the best way to begin explorations to the area.

From Bell Station, walkers should get onto Sandham Road, on the east side of the railway line, and proceed to walk north. About a third of a kilometre up the road there is a fire trail on the east side; this is shown on the Mt Wilson topographic map as a short road that branches off at forty-five degrees and comes to an end at a house. However, it actually passes the house and continues for about five kilometres in a roughly north-east direction before coming to an end just above the Wallangambe River. It has no name that I know of, but I will call it the Wallangambe Trail for convenience. Please note that this trail, where it branches off Sandham Road, is little more than wheel ruts in the grass, and is easily missed; you may have to scout around a bit to find it. About half a kilometre further up Sandham Road you will notice a house with a swing consisting of a tyre suspended from a tree; if you reach this house, you have overshot the mark.

Once you are on the Wallangambe Trail, however, it soon becomes clearer and is easy to follow as it passes the house and continues through the dry eucalypt scrub. After about four kilometres the trail crosses an unnamed creek that flows east to the Wallangambe. Just before the creek, on the east side of the trail there is a clearing that makes a good camp-site. For anyone who intends to spend the night up on the crest somewhere this side of the Wallangambe River, this creek is the place to get water before continuing. On the north side of the creek, the trail goes alongside a minor gully before coming up onto the crest at a point which would be roughly 493918 on the Wallangambe topographic map. It is a pity this trail is not shown on the map, since it is a major access route to this area; but this is not the only problem with this map, as will soon become clear.

Where the trail comes to the top of the crest, there are some interesting, craggy rock formations on the east side, and these are quite characteristic of the area. You cannot go far in this area without seeing quite a few jagged rocks like these ones. From this point, the trail continues roughly north for about a kilometre and comes to an end at some very rocky slopes overlooking the Wallangambe River. From the end of the trail, it is not difficult to clamber down the slopes to have a look at the river, although there is not much to see when you get there. The area is too scrubby for camping, and li-loing is out of the question because of the shallowness of the river and the amount of debris cluttering it. On the north side of the river it is virtually sheer cliff, and this is where the Wallangambe topographic map is one of the most misleading maps I have ever seen. To look at the contour lines around this part of the river, you would think that the slopes on both sides are quite gradual and negotiable; in fact they are sheer cliff most of the way along the river, including along this particular stretch. I am not aware of any passes on the north side of the spot where the trail

Jagged rock formations on the way to the   The Wallangambe River, showing the rugged
Wallangambe River   walls that are so characteristic of the area

ends, so having gone down to the river you would simply have to come back up again.

For anyone who wants to explore the area further, the natural way is to go directly east along the crest from where the first rock formations were found (493918). From this point it is only about one and a half kilometres to the Wallangambe, walking almost in a straight line along the ridge, which is quite clear and easily negotiated. On the other side of the river is the Wallangambe Crater, as shown on the topographic map. You will see that the river flows north-south at this point, with a sharp bend a bit further upstream (509924, Wallangambe). On both sides of this bend, for about a quarter of a kilometre upstream and downstream, the cliffs give way to some more gradual slopes, and this is the simplest place to cross the river if you wish to go further east. Once on the other side, by bearing east around the top rim of the Wallangambe Crater you could head further east along the ridge in the general direction of Lost Flat Mountain, Short Creek and the junction of the Wallangambe and Bungleboori Creek. However, this area is characterised by vague, meandering ridges where it is easy to take wrong turns, so that a walk in that direction is strictly for very good navigators only.

On the other hand, for an easier trip you could simply follow the spur directly north of the bend in the river (509924), and either head for Yarramun Creek or else bear north-west in a broad arc to join the fire trail on the next spur to the west. This fire trail is shown on the map and is easily seen from the spur north of the bend — I will call it the Clarence Trail for convenience. It heads to Lithgow via the Clarence Colliery road and joins the Glow-worm Tunnel Road outside Lithgow (another turn-off near the Clarence Colliery goes down to Chifley Road, east of Lithgow). About five kilometres west along the Clarence Trail, you will note that there is a minor branch that goes north-east to the upper reaches of Dumbano Creek, and places like this, as well as the spur where the Clarence Trail comes to an end, could make good places to set up a base camp from which to do day-walks around the area. This might be one of the easy ways to get to know the place.

My own explorations of this area have only extended a couple of kilometres east of the Wallangambe Crater. I have found the ridges to be very clear and easy to walk along; so clear, in fact, that at times it is like being in someone's paddock (it may, of course, be less clear as the years go by). Although the area is virtually untouched, you do not always feel completely cut off from civilisation, because from the ridges you can see the blessings of civilisation in the distance. The Clarence Colliery is clearly visible from the Wallangambe Trail, where it comes onto the crest, and some of the development along the Bell Range can readily be made out in the distance. At night you can hear the noise of the trains going to or from Lithgow, although this is no doubt less true as you get further east into the heart of the Wallangambe Wilderness.

These notes can only serve as a very basic introduction to an interesting area; anyone who wants to explore the possibilities of this wilderness area would do well to contact a bushwalking club and team up with experienced walkers who already have some knowledge of the Wallangambe Wilderness and who know how to navigate.

3. Deep Pass

Deep Pass is situated right on the northern boundaryof the Blue Mountains National Park, straddling the southern edges of the Wollemi National Park. This area is a further extension of the Wallangambe Wilderness and opens up some very heavy, mountainous country that can be quite fascinating but which is, beyond doubt, strictly for experienced bushwalkers who are *very* skilled at navigation. If the Wallangambe Wilderness is the kind of place where it is easy to take wrong turns, the same can be said of the area around and beyond Deep Pass, and said a thousand times over. From Deep Pass,

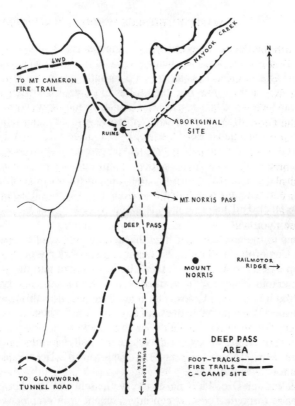

N

TO MT CAMERON
FIRE TRAIL

4WD

NAYOOK CREEK

RUINS
C

ABORIGINAL
SITE

MT. NORRIS PASS

DEEP PASS

MOUNT
NORRIS

RAILMOTOR
RIDGE →

TO BUNGLEBOORI
CREEK

DEEP PASS
AREA
FOOT-TRACKS ----
FIRE TRAILS ▬▬▬
C - CAMP SITE

TO GLOWWORM
TUNNEL ROAD

there is walking access to Mt Norris, which is the beginning of Railmotor Ridge, which in turn meanders eastwards towards the junction of Nayook Creek and the Wallangambe River. By this time we are already into the heavy territory of the Wollemi, a fascinating but rather awesome place that needs to be treated with respect. The Wollemi is the second-largest national park in New South Wales, extending all the way from Deep Pass to the Hunter Valley; it is way beyond the scope of this book and deserves a book of its own.

Further east of Nayook Creek is Clews Range, which stretches to the junction of the Wallangambe River and the legendary Colo River. From the Colo, there are passes that permit access to the Putty Road, making it possible to do some interesting long walks. Anyone interested in getting to know this area should contact bushwalking clubs through the Wilderness Society, 57 Liverpool Street, Sydney, and team up with experienced walkers who preferably know the area or at least have an idea where the passes are. They should also acquire the sketch map of the Colo, which shows the passes around the Colo Gorge and is available at Paddy Pallins.

On the south side of Deep Pass is a network of rugged gullies that link up to form Bungleboori Creek, which flows east to the Wallangambe; on the north side is an equally rugged gully that gives rise to Nayook Creek, which also goes east to join the Wallangambe a bit further downstream from Bungleboori Creek. Deep Pass itself is a pleasantly green and ferny gully that runs north-south, connecting the gullies of Nayook and Bungleboori Creeks. It can be reached by fire trails that branch off the Glow-worm Tunnel Road, an extension of Atkinson Road, Lithgow. About twenty kilometres up the Glow-worm Tunnel Road you come to a large, three-way fork; on the west side there is a turn-off with a locked gate and a sign saying 'No Entry'; this goes to Newnes Afforestation Camp. Ignoring this and the road to the north, take the eastern turn-off and you can follow the fire trails to Deep Pass, but there are many turn-offs along the way and it is necessary to have the Rock Hill topographic map.

On the map you will notice that one trail goes directly to Deep Pass and another goes to the north side of it, near Nayook Creek, after branching off the Mt Cameron Fire Trail. The former trail peters out on the slopes above Deep Pass, and a foot-track then continues down into the pass and turns north to join the trail at the northern end. A minor off-shoot branches south towards Bungleboori Creek; I have not tried to follow this track very far, but I suspect that it probably does not go far before fizzling out in jungle-like undergrowth, as is the case with another track up at Nayook Creek. Anyone going to Deep Pass by car must take the trail that branches off the Mt Cameron Fire Trail, but it gets very rough towards Deep Pass and is strictly for four-wheel drives.

The track through Deep Pass makes a very pleasant walk of about fifteen minutes or so, through a cool, green environment with graphic worm's-eye views of the rugged cliffs of Mt Norris, on the east side of the pass. Where the track joins the trail at the north end, there is a very large grassy area that is excellent for camping. The upper end of Nayook Creek winds around the east edge of this camp ground, providing plenty of water at the time of writing. If the place is a bit drier in future, water could probably be found further downstream.

On the east side of the clearing you will see a sign saying 'Deep Pass Aboriginal Site 500 Metres'. There is a track at this spot that follows Nayook Creek, initially sticking very close to the cliff on the north-west face of Mt Norris. When you come to a long stretch of sandy ground along the foot of the cliff, you are in the vicinity of the Aboriginal site, but I personally was unable to find it; it is, of course, not sign-posted. Later, I was told by a National Parks and Wildlife Service ranger that the site consists of hand stencils on the cliff, but they are hidden behind a boulder. This may be just as well, given the existence of certain people who cannot see something like this without getting the urge to deface it.

Whether you have any luck in finding the hand stencils or not, you may still find it rewarding to follow the track further downstream and have a closer look at Nayook Creek and its surroundings. The track follows the cliff a bit further, getting rougher and narrower as it goes along, and gradually winds its way down to the creek. There is at least one minor turn-off along the way, but it is hard to tell how much of it is a track and how much is simply a natural gap, or series of gaps. It goes nowhere in particular, in any case. Ignoring it, continue down to the creek, which is part of a very lush, densely vegetated world full of fern trees, moss-covered logs and vines. It is quite beautiful, although once the track fizzles out it would be difficult to walk much further; I will not say it cannot be done, but it would be very slow going.

The clearing, apart from being a good place to camp, is also the site of some old stone ruins, which make a picturesque focal-point for the area. I was told there used to be a hut nearby, which may have been the hut shown on the topographic map, but apparently some pyromaniac put a match to it. On the south side of the camp ground, about five minutes' walk back down through the pass, there is a negotiable slope that permits access to Mt Norris, via a section where the slopes are gradual enough to be climbed. It is not marked and the only way I can identify it is as follows: walk south down the track from the camp ground for about five minutes and look for a spot on the east side where the rocky slopes look gradual enough to be clambered up. Ascending the slopes, you pass close to a minor watercourse and gradually find yourself on some reasonably clear, grassy slopes before getting into the timber on the crest of Mt Norris.

The scrub on Mt Norris must constitute one of the unloveliest and most uninviting places I have seen in the Blue Mountains. The dry, eucalypt forest, with scattered banksias, is about as barren and scrubby as scrub can get. There is certainly not much to see, although it has the simple virtue of being the beginning of the wilderness. Anyone who wanted to do an overnight walk up here would have the place to himself and know he was well away from civilisation, which is ultimately what bushwalking is all about. However, as I said before, only experienced walkers should try to go far in this area; even people who do day-walks up to Mt Norris would be well advised to keep their bearings. Furthermore, anyone who wants to do a camping trip up around Mt Norris or other parts of Railmotor Ridge should take a rope for pack-hauling, since the slopes from Deep Pass can be quite steep in places. In closing, I should add that, although Deep Pass may look like the kind of place where you would have it all to yourself, four-wheel drive convoys sometimes call in on weekends, making it advisable, as usual, to go there on a weekday if possible. Anyone who does will have the chance to explore an unusual and interesting place that has a touch of that particular magic that hangs around places off the beaten track.

6. Coxs River to Wollondilly River

The southern part of the park extends to the banks of the Wollondilly River, west of Mittagong. This part of the park was the scene for its fair share of historical developments starting from the days when the early explorers trekked west from the Burragorang Valley. The valley was not, of course, underwater in those days, and as the colony spread west this area became significant as the site of numerous through-routes. The Old Cedar Road extended from the Burragorang Valley to the cedar-getters' trail along Gingra Creek; farms sprang up along Scotts Main Range; the Old Oberon Stock Route linked the area up in a broad arc from the Burragorang Valley to Oberon; and Yerranderie developed as a mining town until its demise in 1930.

The flooding of the valley by the construction of Warragamba Dam, however, cut the access from the Camden and Picton areas and homesteads went into decline all through the region. The properties down Scotts Main Range are now merely ruins, while the area around Yerranderie is dotted with abandoned farms. A few properties still survive around the Bindook Highlands and Bullnigang Heights, but much of the area is now part of the Blue Mountains National Park, and provides considerable scope for those who like to get off the beaten track.

The Old Cedar Road is linked with Coxs River by a steep track down Mt Cookem and with Kanangra by the track along the Gingra Range. The Uni Rover Trail also links Kanangra with the Yerranderie area, and a series of old fire trails fan out towards the Wollondilly River around Mt Egan and New Yards Hill. Vehicular access is restricted to the Old Oberon Stock Route, but anyone prepared to walk will find an area that, while not untouched, is a perfect place to get away from civilisation.

1. Mt Cookem

Mt Cookem can be reached by going to Coxs River from Medlow Gap. A service road goes for about seven kilometres from Medlow Gap to Kelpie Point, on Coxs River, at which stage it fizzles out near a weir and gauging station. From the end of the road, an intermittent foot-track proceeds downstream along the river for about one and a half kilometres, sometimes going along grassy slopes and sometimes giving way to rocks alongside the river, necessitating some clambering but not of a difficult nature. Where the river starts to bend east around Mt Cookem, wade through the water,

Coxs River where it winds around Mt Cookem

which is rarely deep, and walk up to the foot of Mt Cookem. You should see a tree with a sign on it saying 'Prohibited Area' and so on; the word 'Trail' is painted on the bark of the tree, although it is hard to read. There is also a white arrow painted on a rock several metres in front of the tree. The area around the river is quite beautiful and it would be worth spending a few days there, exploring the place.

A few metres or so behind the tree, you will find the track up the mountain, although it may be slightly obscured at first by bushes. Further up, it gets much clearer and there are no problems, apart from energy. This is quite a steep walk which took me about an hour and a half with backpack, including a couple of stops for a break. At the top, the track joins the fire trail down Scotts Main Range; a small cairn marks the trackhead. There are said to be excellent views if you go to the bottom of the trail, where it ends in a loop on Mt Cookem, and then down the slope several metres.

2. Scotts Main Range

From Mt Cookem, the fire trail proceeds about twenty-six kilometres or so down Scotts Main Range. This provides walking access to Yerranderie and the Colong Caves, making it possible to do some interesting extended walks of some days' duration. The walking is easy and straightforward, and provides a strong sense of having the world to yourself, because you can see into the distance both to the east and west, and know there is no civilisation anywhere around. A number of features are encountered along the way, and there is adequate water in the form of six waterholes scattered down the range.

After walking for a couple of hours through some very pleasant forest of pines and eucalypt, you come to the first distinguishing feature: the turn-off where the Old Cedar Road goes down to Lake Burragorang. This road used to go from the cedar-getters' trail, along Gingra Creek, to the Burragorang Valley, but at the latter end it now goes into the prohibited zone around the lake. On the west side of the fire trail, roughly opposite the Cedar Road turn-off, is an abandoned property. You will see the fences as you approach, and just slightly south of the turn-off you will find the remains of Kowmung House. These consist largely of a stone fire-place, bits of corrugated iron, fences and an old water-tank. There is plenty of open space for camping around here, but no water at this stage.

About half an hour's walk further south, you come to the turn-off for New Yards, which is now connected with the Catholic Bushwalking Club and is no relation to New Yards Hill near the Wollondilly River (there are a lot of New Yards around). At the turn-off for New Yards you will find the first of the six waterholes, which may look a little black but can be used if boiled or chlorinated. The presence of water makes this a good place to camp; there is plenty of open space alongside the road, and this is the case all the way down the range.

About a kilometre and a half further down, you pass the second waterhole, which is on the east side of the trail. Half an hour later, you reach a large intersection where the Old Cedar Road goes down to the Kowmung River — this is a popular way of walking to Kanangra, after picking up the track along the Gingra Range. At the intersection on Scotts Main Range, there is another waterhole; this one is very black, but could still be used if treated suitably. Also at this intersection are the remains of Bran Jan House. They can best be found by going down the turn-off to the Kowmung for about a hundred metres, at which point you will see a minor turn-off on your left. What is left of the house is near this turn-off, but there is not much more than fences and posts, a couple of water-tanks, old bits of iron and some pieces of cement sticking out of the ground. Near the turn-off there is a good clearing where you could camp.

A kilometre or so further south along the range, you pass the fourth waterhole, and a couple more are found along the way to Mt Feld, which is about nine kilometres further south. Through this part of the walk there is not a lot of variety, but on the south side of Mt Feld the scenery opens up and provides some views across Kanangra-Boyd National Park, looking generally towards Arabanoo Peak and the ridges south of Kanangra Walls. After that, the distant shape of Kowmung Mountain becomes the dominant feature as you get towards the bottom end of the range, where the trail finally

bears east to go through Byrnes Gap and on to Yerranderie. Note that trail-
bikers sometimes come through here, making their headquarters at some
private property in Byrnes Gap, but this is usually on weekends.

3. Yerranderie

Yerranderie is an old abandoned mining town to the west of Lake
Burragorang and would once have been accessible from Picton, before the
Burragorang Valley was flooded. Nowadays it can only be reached by car
from Oberon, along the long and tortuous Old Oberon Stock Route, placing
it about a hundred kilometres from Oberon. The only other way to reach
it is on foot, the main approaches being via Scotts Main Range or the Uni
Rover Trail from Kanangra Walls Road. Experienced walkers looking for
long walks could also consider going from Thirlmere Lakes and around
Lake Burragorang, for which a permit would have to be obtained from the
Water Board. I have been told that, for those looking for an easier way
to do it, the Chester Bus Company runs package tours to Yerranderie on
a fortnightly basis.

The town was closed in 1930 when world mineral prices made it
uneconomical, and there is still some doubt about whether it could be
economically viable, due to the mines being flooded. However, the whole
town has been bought by a woman named Val Lhuede, who has tried to
develop it as a tourist centre and total environment project. The old post
office is now known as the Lodge and serves as a guest house as well as
home for the caretakers. Visitors can stay at the Lodge and be taken on
tours around the ruins and abandoned mines. There is also a camp ground
on the east side of town, which is run by the Water Board and where people
can camp for free. The town is, of course, full of old mines as well as
abandoned buildings, and visitors can go sightseeing around all these places
in addition to walking in the bush. There is considerable scope for walks,
both long and short, with Yerranderie Peak being one of the most popular.
On the east side of town, past the Water Board camp ground, another track
continues towards Tonalli Pass, which provides what may be the only access
to the tablelands on the west side of Lake Burragorang. These tablelands
— Tonalli, Lacys and Bimlow — are relatively unknown and unexplored,
and provide considerable scope for experienced walkers, although there
could be problems with water.

Anyone interested in Yerranderie could phone 046 596165 to get more
information from the Lodge.

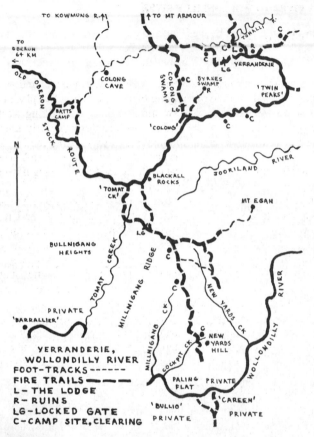

TO KOWMUNG R.

↑ TO MT ARMOUR

TO
OBERON
6+ KM
←

OLD OBERON STOCK ROUTE

COLONG CAVE

BATTS CAMP

N
↑

'TOMAT CK'

BULLNIGANG HEIGHTS

PRIVATE
'BARRALLIER'

COLONG SWAMP

BYRNES SWAMP
R

LG

'COLONG'

BLACKALL ROCKS

TOMAT CREEK

MILLNIGANG RIDGE

TOMALLI

C

C

C

LG

YERRANDERIE

LG

R

C

'TWIN PEAKS'

C

C

C

C

JOORILAND RIVER

MT EGAN

LG

C

C

MILLNIGANG CK

COCKPIT CK

NEW YARDS CK

C

NEW YARDS HILL

PALING FLAT

'BULLIO'
PRIVATE

PRIVATE

'CAREEN'
PRIVATE

WOLLONDILLY RIVER

YERRANDERIE,
WOLLONDILLY RIVER
FOOT-TRACKS ------
FIRE TRAILS — — —
L- THE LODGE
R- RUINS
LG-LOCKED GATE
C-CAMP SITE, CLEARING

Yerranderie Peak, seen from the grounds of the old church

4. Colong Swamp

Colong Swamp is several kilometres west of Yerranderie and offers an interesting day-walk for anyone staying there, or an attractive place to camp for anyone passing through. The swamp is reached by walking west along the fire trail at the back of the Lodge, passing through fairly uneventful eucalypt forest for about eight kilometres before reaching the Mt Armour fire trail. About halfway along — ie about four kilometres from Yerranderie — there are a couple of clearings that could be used for camping if necessary, although there is not much by way of water.

When you reach the Mt Armour trail, it is worth noting that, to the west, there is a track to Colong Cave, which in turn links up with the Uni Rover Trail to Kanangra Walls Road. However, for the present walk, turn south-east and after a kilometre of fairly scrubby bush you come to the Colong Swamp area, where the bush opens up and becomes very pleasant, with grey gums, cliffs in the background and quite probably some kangaroos. This is a good place to spend a night if anyone is interested in camping trips, and there would usually be some water around.

A little further south, the trail turns east and fords Colong Creek, which is quite deep at this point and should provide a reliable supply of water. Continuing for a couple of kilometres further south, you come to a gate on the edge of the 'Colong' property, where you may see some cattle grazing. From this gate, another trail goes north-east to join the main road from Yerranderie. Just before the main road, there is a minor turn-off that goes to the ruins at Byrnes Swamp, as shown on the Bindook topographic map. The track to Byrnes Swamp gets quite vague towards the end and needs to be followed very carefully, but the ruins are, in any case, rather meagre: just bits of iron and a bed-frame. It is hardly worth going out of your way for, although it gives an insight into the very special kind of person it would take to lead such an isolated existence.

Once back on the main road to Yerranderie, it is about twelve kilometres back to town, passing through basically eucalypt forest with the cliffs of the Peaks looming over the north side of the road. There are occasional clearings where camping would be possible, between the Colong Swamp trail and the spot known as the Gap. East of the Gap, you pass an abandoned property called 'Twin Peaks', opposite which there are some views of Lake Burragorang between the trees. After that, the road turns north-west to Yerranderie, making a round-trip of about twenty-six kilometres. Fit walkers could do this in a day, but the caretaker at the Lodge told me they could arrange to pick people up — from near the 'Colong' property, for example — if they were guests at the Lodge. An attractive alternative would be to camp at Colong Swamp and do day-walks around the area. In either case, the Yerranderie and Bindook topographic maps are worth having.

5. New Yards Hill Area

On the south side of the road to Yerranderie there are some fire trails that open up some interesting places for those who like to get off the beaten track. Just west of Blackall Rocks, which are shown on the Bindook map, there is a fire trail that branches off the main road and goes south for about two kilometres. It is shown on the CMA map of the Blue Mountains and Burragorang — which is well worth having — but was left off the Bindook map. The trail joins the one that goes from the 'Tomat Creek' property to Mt Egan. Unfortunately, I have never got around to Mt Egan but, about one and a half kilometres along the Mt Egan trail, there is a branch that goes south to the area around New Yards Hill, overlooking the Wollondilly River. The trail winds along the ridges for about seven kilometres, eventually coming to an end at a dip in the hills just south-west of New Yards Hill. There may be a few roos around, and the area gives you the feeling of being remote from civilisation and of having the bush to yourself.

There are a few good clearings along the way that can serve as campsites. The first is a small clearing about half a kilometre down the trail, on the west side. The second is a better clearing about two kilometres down, again on the west side. Another is where the trail crosses the upper part of Cockpit Creek, just west of New Yards Hill. There is plenty of open space around here and always at least a bit of water, even if it is stagnant and has to be boiled or chlorinated. This spot could make a good base camp for anyone who wanted to spend a few days in the area and do day-walks around the hills and down to the Wollondilly. It is not hard to walk down the slopes to the river; the hills are reasonably steep but often fairly clear and not difficult to negotiate. The Wollondilly River, which forms part of the boundary of the Blue Mountains National Park, is a beautiful place to walk around or camp. Much of the area is, unfortunately, private property, but if you avoid these spots there are some beautiful places to see. There is very little public access to this part of the river, except by walking down from the hills. One access point is at Goodmans Ford Bridge, where the Wombeyan Caves Road crosses the Wollondilly. There are clearings that can be used for camping on both sides of the river, just downstream of the bridge. The clearing on the east side of the river is quite accessible but gets flogged to death, and is virtually devoid of firewood; best avoided. On the west side, there are rougher clearings in the vicinity of Jocks Creek, serviced by a jeep track that branches off the Caves Road.

Anyone who walks down to the river from around New Yards Hill may arrive at Paling Flat; please note that this is private property and camping is absolutely not tolerated. The land on the south side of the river is also private property; anyone interested in access should first contact the owners of 'Bullio' or 'Careen' properties, Bullio, Wombeyan Caves Road, via Mittagong. These are pastoral properties and unscheduled bushwalkers could be in danger of arriving at inappropriate times and getting in the way. I might add that I have found the owners of these properties to be highly cooperative and civilised people, so the cooperation of bushwalkers in this matter would be greatly appreciated by the owners as well as the author.

Camping is possible west of Paling Flat, between Cockpit Creek and Tomat Creek, since this area is part of the national park, apart from a pocket of land at Apple Tree Flat. The map of the Blue Mountains and Burragorang shows all the boundaries of the park.

6. Kanangra

Kanangra-Boyd National Park is worth a book in its own right and is, unfortunately, somewhat beyond the scope of this book. However, some of the main tracks in the park link up with tracks in the southern part of the Blue Mountains National Park, and it is worth giving some attention to them. With a bit of planning and imagination, some exciting walks can be devised that enable experienced walkers to get away from civilisation for days on end, while beginners and those with only moderate experience will find that there are simpler walks that can be done, and which provide the opportunity to see some of the most spectacular scenery in the mountains. Although Kanangra is not part of the Blue Mountains National Park, it could just as easily have been incorporated in the same park, since it is an extension of the same country. The main feature is the Kanangra Grand Gorge and, most particularly, Kanangra Walls, the spectacular cliff formation that looks over the gorge. *Kanangra* is an Aboriginal word meaning beautiful view, and if you go there you will see how it got its name.

The lookout providing the best views can be reached via Kanangra Walls Road, which in turn can be reached via Jenolan or Oberon. At the end of Kanangra Walls Road there is a car-park, from which a walking track leads to Echo Head, which provides the view of the gorge and Kanangra Walls. Part of the way down this track there used to be a rouch picnic area, but this was eliminated recently when the track was restored and upgraded. The track is now in very good condition — at the time of writing, of course — but, alas, we have lost our picnic area. At the end of the track, however, you will find an excellent vantage point from which you have a great view

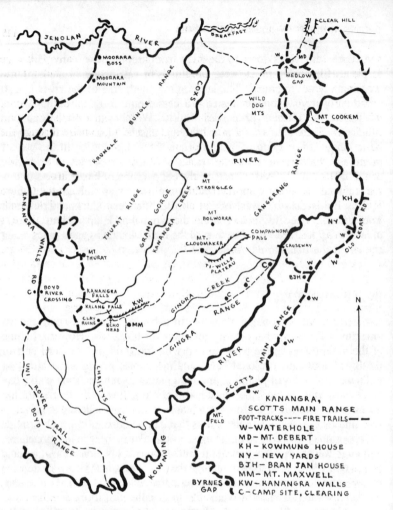

KANANGRA,
SCOTTS MAIN RANGE
FOOT-TRACKS ---- FIRE TRAILS ━━━
W—WATERHOLE
MD—MT. DEBERT
KH—KOWMUNG HOUSE
NY—NEW YARDS
BJH—BRAN JAN HOUSE
MM—MT. MAXWELL
KW—KANANGRA WALLS
C—CAMP SITE, CLEARING

of the gorge and walls. In the distance, if you know where to look, you can make out Clear Hill and the Narrow Neck Plateau, while at night the lights of Sydney can be seen.

Near the lookout, you will see a sign-posted track to the west, which leads down to Kanangra Brook, where there are cascades and a decent pool to drink from and have a dip in. If you walk upstream for fifty metres or so you will find Kalang Falls, which are quite beautiful. At the top of the track you can get a glimpse of Kanangra Falls, a bit further to the north, but only the top part of them. The track down to the brook is rougher than the main track to Echo Head, so that anyone going there should wear something sensible on their feet, which I mention because many people go to places like this without being prepared for a rough track and without wearing suitable footwear.

On the way to Echo Head you will also pass a track on the east side, which leads to Mt Maxwell, which the bulk of Kanangra Walls are a part of. The track continues for about three-quarters of a kilometre through the heath that is characteristic of this area, and goes close to the cliffs, at which point it is worth leaving the main track for a moment to get a closer look at the walls and the rugged ridges around the gorge. From around here, the track bends south along the heath of Mt Maxwell to reach the Gingra Range. It then follows the range for about twelve kilometres and descends to the junction of Gingra Creek and the Kowmung River, where there is a rough camp-site. There are also some clearings among the pines along the last few kilometres of the Gingra Range. From the junction of Gingra Creek and the Kowmung, a scrappy jeep track leads to a causeway that crosses the river to join the Old Cedar Road, thus making it possible to do some extended walks between Kanangra, Scotts Main Range and ultimately Katoomba or, in the other direction, Yerranderie.

From Mt Maxwell, a continuation of the main track also goes further east along the Gangerang Range and out to Mt Cloudmaker, the highest peak on the range. I have not gone out this way myself, but I have been told that it is about half a day's walk from Kanangra Walls to Cloudmaker, from where it is possible to continue in various directions. One possibility is to go to Mt Strongleg and then down to Coxs River; another is to turn south-east at Cloudmaker and go down to the Ti-Willa Plateau, the expansive plateau that can be seen from various points around the Jamison Valley. Features of the plateau are the Hundred Man Cave, facing Mt Cloudmaker and so-called because it is reportedly big enough to house one hundred men (feminists please note that this author did not invent the name); and the Compagnoni Pass, at the north-east tip of the plateau. This pass is said to be equipped with chains and provides access to the slopes leading down to the Kowmung River, and thence the Old Cedar Road. This area is, of course, strictly for experienced walkers, who should invest in the 'Gangerang' map if they want to get more details of these places, since much of this information is not shown on the topographic maps.

Camping is prohibited at Echo Head, but there is a large camp ground at the Boyd River Crossing, about seven kilometres back along Kanangra Walls Road. This camp ground is equipped with fire-places, wood and toilets. For those who like to rough it, there are some rudimentary camp-sites on the north side of Kanangra Walls Road, about half a kilometre before its end. In the same vicinity there are some ruins known as the Clay House Ruins, but there is not much left of them.

Five or six kilometres west from Echo Head is the entrance to the Uni Rover Trail, which goes about fifteen kilometres along the Boyd Range to reach the Kowmung River. From the river, the track continues south to Colong Cave and then forks, with one branch going to Colong Swamp and another to Batts Camp, a well known Kanangra camp-site off the Old Oberon Stock Route. These tracks make it possible for fit walkers to plan some long walks around the area; one possibility would be to walk down the Uni Rover Trail, up Scotts Main Range, down to the Kowmung River, along the Gingra Range and back up to Kanangra Walls Road via Mt Maxwell — a round trip of about eighty kilometres, partly in the Blue Mountains National Park and partly in Kanangra.

7. Burragorang Lookout

This lookout is not exactly an example of bushwalking and is not even in the Blue Mountains, but is too good to leave out and provides views of parts of the Blue Mountains which would otherwise be inaccessible to most people. It is situated about twenty-two kilometres west of Camden and can be approached via the Burragorang Road, passing through the Oaks and Nattai. At Nattai — which was discovered by Barrallier and served as his base camp — a sign-posted road turns up to the lookout, where you will find a kiosk, picnic facilities and fire-places.

From the lookout there are superb views of Lake Burragorang, looking both north and south, and the mountains and tablelands of the southern part of the Blue Mountains National Park. Directly west are the Tonalli Tablelands; to the north-west, parts of the Bimlow Tablelands are visible; to the south is the Wollondilly River and other features like Tonalli Cove, the Wanganderry Walls and even Mt Egan, which can be discerned if you do a bit of orienting with map and compass. It is also possible to make out Mt Cloudmaker to the west, although it is just a bump on the horizon. At night you can see the lights of Katoomba without any trouble.

This view is particularly good in the late afternoon, when the sun's rays stream across the tablelands and the lake, and in the twilight. Early in the morning, you could be lucky enough to catch the mist over the lake, as I did one day at 5.30 am. A yellow, full moon was going down over yellow cliffs, the lake was covered in mist and the sky was pink; it looked like another planet.

Unfortunately, there is not much by way of public transport to the area. A school bus goes to Nattai in the morning, and the nearest railway station is at Campbelltown. There is a shop at Nattai as well as the kiosk at the lookout.

Index